Quantifying the Qualitative

To Parents

Quantifying the Qualitative

Information Theory for Comparative Case Analysis

Katya Drozdova

Seattle Pacific University

Kurt Taylor Gaubatz

Old Dominion University

Los Angeles | London | New Delhi
Singapore | Washington DC

Los Angeles | London | New Delhi
Singapore | Washington DC

FOR INFORMATION:

SAGE Publications, Inc.
2455 Teller Road
Thousand Oaks, California 91320
E-mail: order@sagepub.com

SAGE Publications Ltd.
1 Oliver's Yard
55 City Road
London, EC1Y 1SP
United Kingdom

SAGE Publications India Pvt. Ltd.
B 1/I 1 Mohan Cooperative Industrial Area
Mathura Road, New Delhi 110 044
India

SAGE Publications Asia-Pacific Pte. Ltd.
3 Church Street
#10–04 Samsung Hub
Singapore 049483

Acquisitions Editor: Vicki Knight
Editorial Assistant: Yvonne McDuffee
Production Editor: Veronica Stapleton
    Hooper
Copy Editor: Gillian Dickens
Typesetter: Hurix Systems
Proofreader: Wendy Jo Dymond
Cover Designer: Anupama Krishnan
Marketing Manager: Nicole Elliott

Copyright © 2017 by SAGE Publications, Inc.

ISBN: 978-1-4833-9247-9

Cover Image Credit: Image: Simulation of Black Hole Flare. Credit: NASA, S. Gezari (The Johns Hopkins University), and J. Guillochon (University of California, Santa Cruz), 2012. Retrieved from http://hubblesite.org/about_us/copyright.php

This book is printed on acid-free paper.

16 17 18 19 20 10 9 8 7 6 5 4 3 2 1

Brief Contents

SAGE was founded in 1965 by Sara Miller McCune to support the dissemination of usable knowledge by publishing innovative and high-quality research and teaching content. Today, we publish over 900 journals, including those of more than 400 learned societies, more than 800 new books per year, and a growing range of library products including archives, data, case studies, reports, and video. SAGE remains majority-owned by our founder, and after Sara's lifetime will become owned by a charitable trust that secures our continued independence.

Los Angeles | London | New Delhi | Singapore | Washington DC

Detailed Contents

List of Tables

List of Figures

Preface

* *

In this book, we set out a new systematic approach to comparative case analysis based on the fundamental insights of information theory. In essence, we present a method for learning more from the information you have and exercising better judgment under conditions of uncertainty, especially in complex environments. Information theory (Shannon, 1948) emerged as a universal way to quantify information content. Meanwhile, advances in comparative case study research in political science (George & Bennett, 2005; George & Smoke, 1974) have tackled complementary issues of how to systematically learn from historical experience and contextualized observations to inform and improve policy decisions. We synthesize core insights from these areas of information and political sciences to develop novel analytic tools with a much broader set of applications to research and practice.

Across a wide range of fields, there has been a significant resurgence of interest in case study methods and multimethod analytics. Our new approach avoids the limitations of traditional statistics in the small-*n* context and allows the analyst to systematically compare and assess the impact of a set of factors on case outcomes with easy-to-use analytics based on well-established ideas about the meaning and measurement of information. These ideas are grounded in applied mathematics, but we present them in a very hands-on way to enhance qualitative research and assess lessons learned.

A central merit of this approach is that it is exceedingly simple and transparent. It is, therefore, practical for a wide range of analysts as well as for practitioners who make difficult and consequential decisions under uncertainty. It is accessible and intuitive for those with a relatively limited background in quantitative analysis. It provides a straightforward metric for comparing factor impacts that can be effectively communicated to a range of readers and leaders. This is a significant virtue in an environment in which quantitative analysis is becoming increasingly esoteric and limited to a small number of scholars with highly advanced training. Qualitative and mixed-methods analysis stands to benefit from more accessible analytic tools that can reduce bias and improve the knowledge gained from comparative case studies.

Who Is This Book For? The Audience for Stronger Case Study Methods

* *

The information techniques we teach in this book are for students, educators, policy makers, researchers, and professionals who need a more rigorous and systematic approach to doing and learning from comparative case studies. It will be most appropriate for those analyzing between 5 and 50 cases. This includes the range below about 30 where traditional statistics often break down.

Quantifying the Qualitative will be useful for any broad-based research or analytical methods course. These nonparametric techniques are valuable not only as an approach to small-*n* research problems but also as a conceptual framework for understanding the relationship between research, information, and action. This book will be of particular use for classes in qualitative analysis or mixed methods. But it will also be helpful for traditional statistics courses where there is an interest in exposing students to alternative approaches for the many instances where large-*N* statistics are inappropriate.

The book should be accessible and appropriate for both undergraduate and graduate students. The techniques we demonstrate in this book require only minimal quantitative skills, and we explain and review all the relevant concepts. The primary computational burden on the user is to be able to count. The calculation of information metrics requires a basic conceptual understanding of logarithms, which we provide in Chapter 2, and the ability to use a spreadsheet or calculator. In Appendix A, we walk through the straightforward use of Excel or Google Sheets for these calculations. We also provide sample Excel spreadsheets on the book website at http://study.sagepub.com/drozdova. Appendix B provides an implementation of the method in the open-source statistical computer language R for readers who prefer that approach.

Policy makers and practitioners, too, will find *Quantifying the Qualitative* useful. It is a truism that information is a critical element for making decisions. Policy makers and other decision analysts have become increasingly focused on evidence-based practices. In many policy arenas, the only available evidence comes from relatively small numbers of observations that often have the basic characteristics of a comparative case study.

Beyond traditional qualitative case studies, this approach also applies to aggregating results and evaluating policy-relevant lessons from multiple empirical studies. Meta-analysis is an increasingly important tool for supporting decisions in many fields (Cooper, Hedges, & Valentine, 2009). Often the individual studies may have sufficient observations for statistical techniques, but the number of studies is relatively few, and the underlying data are unavailable or incommensurable. The information metrics we present can facilitate a more systematic and rigorous understanding of the aggregated results of diverse studies to identify broader policy implications or actionable findings.

The approach that we advance in this book puts the focus on understanding and objectively assessing the information content of case studies. The method we set out is both conceptually and technically accessible. Throughout the book, we reach out to provide examples and approaches that will be of particular interest to policy makers.

Features and Benefits: How to Use This Book

The methods set out in *Quantifying the Qualitative* will allow qualitative researchers to more effectively design, understand, and present the results of comparative case studies. It will be of benefit to instructors, students, and professional users.

Quantifying the Qualitative presents a new and powerful technique to allow case study researchers to make their work more rigorous, systematic, and reproducible. This book is unique in that there are no other available and easily accessible approaches for the systematic and reproducible assessment of comparative case studies.

Quantifying the Qualitative is a path-breaking work both in its application of information theory to enhance comparative case study methods and also for introducing information theory to a much broader audience. The social sciences, in particular, have underappreciated the power and applicability of information theory—a body of knowledge that was the motive force for the digital revolution. We draw on a number of social science examples, as well as examples from medicine, education, and ecology, to demonstrate the application of information metrics to comparative case studies. From a practical perspective, our approach applies to a variety of problems where evaluating the observable characteristics of a situation may be informative about an unknown outcome of interest. For example, it is especially apt for evaluating strategies, indicators and warnings in defense, diplomacy, counterterrorism, military, intelligence, and law enforcement applications but also broadly in business, health care, environmental policy, and other settings where consequential decisions are made under conditions of uncertainty and complexity. Our approach can help you make better decisions.

The methods we introduce here are described in careful detail. We provide both a clear explication of the background concepts and theory, as well as a step-by-step guide to implementing this approach. This includes a thorough tutorial in Appendix A on using Excel for conducting information analysis and online resources at http://study.sagepub.com/drozdova.

For users who are familiar with R, we have provided a set of R functions in Appendix B, as well as the complete R code for reproducing everything in the book (available at http://study .sagepub.com/drozdova).

Teaching Case Studies: A Note for Instructors

Quantifying the Qualitative gives you a powerful tool to share with your students who are interested in pursuing small-*n* research. It can be particularly useful for students who have time or other constraints that make collection of small-*n* data more manageable than the creation of large-*N* data sets. Undergraduates, in particular, should be able to learn these straightforward techniques, collect appropriate data, and analyze them in the course of a semester or a yearlong thesis project. Master's, doctoral, or professional education students could readily use the techniques for their studies or work.

The basic information theory techniques can be understood and implemented with a minimal sense of algebra. They offer not only concrete and simple analytic tools for case studies but also—for those with enquiring minds—many exciting and intellectually motivating insights into the fundamental basis of our Information Age and the preceding Cold War era of nuclear physics and spy games, which made uncertainty evermore consequential and information theory somewhat of a lifesaver and a game-changer. But these concepts can also be used to open doors into other areas. For example, probability concepts, the Bayesian perspective, research design, and the logic of inference could all be taught starting from information-theoretic foundations. Information theory can also provide a stepping stone into the philosophy and concepts of *qualitative case analysis* (QCA), as we discuss in Chapter 7.

Because the techniques are so straightforward, students can be up and running with projects very quickly. This gives the instructor significant leverage for teaching a wide variety of research design issues. Students can see how these issues resonate in their own research projects so that research design can be taught in a concrete and motivated real-world context from the beginning, rather than waiting for students to learn sufficient statistics to take on their own projects.

The Bottom Line

Comparative case studies remain a critical tool for policy making and scholarship. The applications of information theory we present in this book significantly enhance case study work by making it more systematic, rigorous, and replicable. Despite being at the cutting edge, these techniques are conceptually intuitive and straightforward to implement. How informative an explanatory factor is about an outcome is precisely what we are looking for in case study research. And we are confident that these techniques are simple enough to be accessible for a wide range of students, educators, policy makers, professionals, and scholars. *If you can count, you can do it.*

Free tools and additional resources are available at http://study.sagepub.com/drozdova.

Acknowledgments

We are particularly grateful to the set of expert reviewers SAGE assembled to assess this project. Martie Gillen (University of Florida), Michael D. Grimes (Louisiana State University), Juanita A. Johnson (Union Institute & University), Frank Lambert (Kent State University), Teresa M. Martinelli (University of La Verne), Mark Meo (University of Oklahoma), Stacee L. Reicherzer (Walden University), Laura Roselle (Elon University and Duke University), Jacob Shively (University of West Florida), Wayne Smith (California State University, Northridge), Shon D. Smith (University of Florida), and Judy R. Van Doorn (Troy University) gave the manuscript a careful read and brought together the perspectives of a wide range of fields. They made a number of suggestions that have improved the final form of this book.

Vicki Knight and her editorial and production team at SAGE have been unfailingly supportive and diligent in seeing this effort to fruition. Their consistent attention and professionalism bear some significant responsibility for the success of this project. It would be difficult to imagine a more effective and responsive publication process.

We also thank our friends and colleagues for their encouragement and support.

Publisher's Acknowledgments

SAGE wishes to acknowledge the following peer reviewers for their editorial insight and guidance:

Martie Gillen, University of Florida

Michael D. Grimes, Louisiana State University

Juanita A. Johnson, Union Institute & University

Frank Lambert, Ph.D., Kent State University

Teresa M. Martinelli, University of La Verne

Mark Meo, University of Oklahoma

Stacee L. Reicherzer, Walden University

Laura Roselle, Elon University and Duke University

Jacob Shively, University of West Florida

Wayne Smith, California State University–Northridge

Shon D. Smith, University of Florida

Judy R. Van Doorn, Troy University

About the Authors

Ekaterina "Katya" Drozdova, PhD, is an assistant professor of political science in the School of Business, Government, and Economics at Seattle Pacific University. She has lectured extensively and taught courses on subjects ranging from research methods in social science to global security, strategy, history, information, and political economy as well as carried out a number of research projects in these areas which successfully utilized both qualitative and quantitative techniques.

Professor Drozdova has earned a PhD and MPhil in Information Systems from New York University's Stern School of Business, Department of Information, Operations, and Management Sciences; as well as an MA in international policy studies and BA in international relations from Stanford University. Her research interests broadly focus on understanding how systemic risks and technology choices help shape operational strategies—with emphasis on organizational threat prevention and response applications in diverse contexts: from countering terrorist networks to securing energy, cyber, and other critical infrastructures.

Katya has been actively involved with leading military, policy, law enforcement, and business professionals in identifying mission-critical challenges and formulating effective global responses across multiple organization risk areas. Her recent work and publications have dealt with issues of US national and international security—specifically addressing the problems of hybrid and asymmetric low-tech threats in the high-tech age—as well as with optimization of organizations' human and technological networks for improved success rate in complex and hostile environments.

Prof. Drozdova is an affiliate with the Empirical Studies of Conflict Project (ESOC) at Stanford and Princeton Universities as well as a principal investigator for the Mining Afghan Lessons from Soviet Era (MALSE) research program, which has been funded by the US Office of the Secretary of Defense's (OSD) Human Social Cultural and Behavioral (HSCB) Sciences program through the Office of Naval Research's (ONR) Expeditionary Maneuver Warfare and Combating Terrorism Department and the Naval Postgraduate School. She has been a fellow at New York University's Alexander Hamilton Center for Political Economy and Stanford University's Hoover Institution on War, Revolution, and Peace as well as Stanford's Center for International Security and Cooperation (CISAC). At CISAC, Katya has also been a member of the Consortium for Research on Information Security and Policy funded by the US National Security Agency (NSA) and comprising leading scholars as well as industry and government practitioners, including former directors of Lawrence Livermore National Laboratory (LLNL) and Defense Advanced Research Projects Agency (DARPA).

Kurt Taylor Gaubatz, PhD, is an associate professor in the Graduate Program in International Studies at Old Dominion University. In addition to courses in international relations and international law, he regularly teaches research methods and advanced statistics. He has previously taught methodology and formal modeling as a faculty member at Stanford University and at Oxford University (Nuffield College), where he was the visiting John G. Winant Lecturer in American Foreign Policy. He has also served as the Susan Luise Dyer Peace Fellow at the Hoover Institution at Stanford University and received a Pew Faculty Fellowship from the Kennedy School of Government at Harvard University.

Professor Gaubatz's most recent book is *A Survivor's Guide to R* (SAGE, 2015), which is a broad and cross-disciplinary introduction to the R language for statistical programming. He is also the author of *Elections and War* (Stanford University Press, 1999), which is a study of the electoral politics of military conflict. His work on international law and on the relationship between domestic politics and international relations has appeared in a number of leading journals. His work on political modeling has received funding from the U.S. Department of Defense.

Professor Gaubatz earned an AB in economics from the University of California at Berkeley, an MALD in international law from the Fletcher School of Law and Diplomacy, an MDiv in theology from Princeton Theological Seminary, and a PhD in political science from Stanford University. More information can be found at kktg.net/kurt.

CHAPTER 1

Enhancing Small-*n* Analysis

Information Theory and the Method of Structured-Focused Comparison

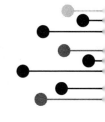

This is "the Information Age." The explosion of digitized information has led to important innovations in scholarship across a broad range of fields. Most of these developments have been focused on the emerging computational technologies for efficiently processing and analyzing "big data," the massive streams of digital information generated by our online lives. At the same time, however, appreciation has grown for the role of smaller, contextualized, and more detail-oriented case study techniques. This renewed focus on case studies is due both to the rise of increasingly complex and exclusionary quantitative techniques and to a better understanding of the promise of mixed methods, of working through problems at different levels of focus. Large-*N* and small-*n* analyses are complementary rather than competitive.

In this book, we argue that the core insights about the nature of information that launched the Information Age can be turned toward the task of enhancing small-*n* analysis. We make the case here for the use of information theory as a powerful but accessible tool for making comparative case studies more rigorous and systematic. It is a powerful approach because it provides rigor and replicability without many of the limitations that arise for traditional statistics in situations with severely limited numbers of observations. It is accessible in that it requires only minimal quantitative skills. As we will demonstrate, these techniques can be easily implemented with a simple spreadsheet program. Indeed, our argument will be that "if you can count, you can do it."

Our approach for conducting case studies scientifically draws on the method of structured-focused comparison. The structured-focused method encourages systematic discipline in comparative case studies, but it lacks rigorous tools for assessing the results. The field of information theory provides straightforward quantitative metrics for assessing uncertainty and knowledge gained from and across cases.

Why Quantify the Qualitative? Enhancing Qualitative Analysis With Information Theory

James Gleick (2011) opens his book, *The Information*, with a story about work at Bell Labs in 1948. That year saw the basic research arm of the Bell Telephone monopoly announce two world-changing innovations. The lesser of these, Gleick argues, was the invention of the transistor. The more important was Claude E. Shannon's 1948 paper, "A Mathematical Theory of Communication." That technical paper set out a mathematical foundation for the unified understanding, communication, and measurement of information regardless of its content. Shannon's paper introduced the world to the term *bit* to refer to a discrete unit for measuring information. This shaped the language of ones and zeros now universal and essential to our Information Age. Shannon's paper also included a simple formula to calculate the minimal number of bits required to accurately communicate any information. Humans had pondered information since time immemorial, but there had not been a universal metric until Shannon's information theory-based measures, *information entropy* and *mutual information*.

Shannon's insights were, in the words of Princeton professor Sergio Verdú (1998), "the Magna Carta of the information age." Mathematician Ian Stewart (2012) includes Shannon's information formula among the seventeen most consequential mathematical equations in history. The computer scientist John MacCormick (2013) identifies Shannon's contribution as one of "Nine Algorithms that Changed the Future." Information theory has since grown as a distinct and highly productive branch of applied mathematics and computer science, with implications across many other disciplines, and it is apt for our new application to case study research.

Across a number of fields, the use of comparative case studies is at a watershed moment. The huge advances in big data (itself a direct consequence of Shannon's revolutionary work) have led to increasingly complex and rarefied quantitative methods. At the same time, there is an increasing appreciation for the complementarity of qualitative and quantitative analysis (Johnson, Onwuegbuzie, & Turner, 2007). Qualitative analysis can help validate and contribute nuance to large-*N* analysis as well as generate new hypotheses or rich contextual explanations. The limitation of qualitative analysis is that it has always been dependent on subjective assessment. The analyst collects data on some set of cases and then uses the natural processing power of the human brain to tease out relevant patterns. Information theory provides an exceedingly straightforward and accessible approach that can make qualitative case comparisons more systematic and reproducible. It can make them more scientific.

The core of all science is to infer something valid about the world from the limited data observed. The scientific role of data analysis, including small-*n* case study work, is to discern the information content of the data. Which variables or factors are most informative about an outcome we wish to study? How much can the available data tell us about a phenomenon of interest? This is essentially an issue of communication—hence the relevance of Claude Shannon's mathematical theory of communication.

In this book, we provide an accessible explanation of Shannon's information concepts and show how they can be effectively applied to make comparative case studies more rigorous and systematic. We demonstrate step-by-step the simple calculation of information metrics to significantly enhance the method of structured-focused case study analysis and the communication of comparative case study results.

Who Needs to Quantify the Qualitative?

This book is for scholars, analysts, and practitioners who need to draw information and insights from relatively modest quantities of data. Many kinds of program analysis and evaluation, for example, might involve small numbers of observations but still require systematic assessment. Policy makers often make consequential decisions based on limited information. Medical researchers interested in the meta-analysis of previously published studies are often challenged to provide clear metrics of aggregation. Scholars across a number of disciplines often conduct more in-depth qualitative study of a set of comparable cases but need to communicate an overarching sense of their findings. In all of these examples and many others, information theory can provide a reproducible metric for systematically understanding the patterns and quality of information contained in qualitative data.

More concretely, the techniques we develop and demonstrate are ideal for working with 4 to 30 comparative cases. For fewer than 4 cases, information theory won't tell you very much that isn't directly observable and will be highly sensitive to changes in any single case. Above about 30 cases, traditional statistical techniques may be as useful, but as we argue, information theory can still provide a powerful measure of uncertainty reduction that does not depend on assumptions about the underlying distribution, is capable of detecting complex relationships that may be overlooked by more traditional central tendency based measures, and can provide a precise measure of independence among variables.

The cases for analysis need to be set up with a single outcome variable and a distinct set of explanatory factors. All of the variables must be amenable to binary coding—that is, to be assigned values of either zero or one. This is straightforward based on systematically measured underlying variables and clear definitions, although developing such definitions to measure complex variables or abstract concepts often explored by qualitative work can be a challenge. The process of clarifying variable definitions and measurements itself carries significant value for case studies independently of information metrics. Cases and conditions that are clearly defined and replicably measured will provide a stronger foundation for drawing inferences, whether through the techniques we outline in this book or even just with traditional qualitative assessment.

Many areas and kinds of study will fall within these broad parameters and have traditionally been the focus of qualitative work. There are numerous advantages to in-depth qualitative and methodologically careful subjective work. Our analytic approach in no way reduces the ability to draw analytic inferences from comparative case studies in the traditional case study mode. Instead, information theory contributes a systematic and reproducible metric to aid in the analysis and communication of analytic results.

Before delving into these powerful new methods, it is helpful to briefly step back and appreciate the broader context and tradition of policy-relevant scholarship—engaging some of the most critical challenges and advancements of the modern era from the advent of nuclear weapons to the Information Age and beyond—that has produced the structured-focused method as well as motivated our approach to enhance it with information analytics.

Information and Action Under Uncertainty

At the dawn of the Information Age, scholars and practitioners were thinking about information and how it is transmitted and communicated. We are interested in how case studies transmit and communicate information, and so it is worth spending a little time on the essential formative story of how the ideas and concepts that we apply here arose from an overarching agenda of applying fundamental science to vital issues. The origins of information theory stretch to the days before the Internet was invented and computing became ubiquitous, the days when social networking still meant talking directly face-to-face. Since then, information theory has helped transform societies and our daily lives through critical scientific and technological achievements.

In the mid-20th century, many scientific efforts coalesced around winning World War II and the uncertain peace that followed in the Cold War. Nuclear weapons became a terrifying reality that coupled basic science and public policy with the risks of mutually assured destruction. The scientific knowledge that went into harnessing the atom also created opportunities for tremendous advancements in human society through the application of new energy, computing, and intellectual resources for peaceful purposes.

Demand for answers to fundamental research questions arose across the many fields that needed to find better ways to process information and manage uncertainty. Physicists, mathematicians, computer scientists, and engineers as well as social scientists adopted this urgent agenda. Its practical applications ranged from breaking enemy codes and avoiding a nuclear war to improving communications and creating the new industries that would give rise to the Information Age. Information theory and the developments in case study methodology that we synthesize in this book both emerged to meet these critical challenges.

Origins and Motivations

Alexander George and the Method of Structured-Focused Comparison

The need for decision making under conditions of uncertainty spurred an interest in the systematic use of case studies across a variety of fields. Such work was essential for effective learning from past experience as well as generating basic knowledge.

Alexander L. George, one of the earliest recipients of a MacArthur Foundation "Genius Grant," was an American political scientist and one of the leading theoreticians for the systematic use of comparative case studies in the social sciences. George coined the term *structured, focused comparison* to designate a form of case study analysis that could compete with large-N analysis for a claim to systematic and scientific status (George & Bennett, 2005). The method of structured-focused comparison is really just a worked-out version of John Stuart Mill's method of agreement and method of difference (Mill, 1843; Van Evera, 1997). The essential element of structured-focused comparison is the use of theory to clearly and explicitly identify a single outcome variable of interest and a set of causal factors. These variables should be defined and measured consistently across a carefully selected set of cases. The combination of theory with a systematic approach to the cases allows for methodologically rigorous empirical investigation.

George spent most of the 1960s as a social scientist at the RAND Corporation. There, he focused on the challenges of interstate conflict and preventing nuclear war. He developed the method of structured-focused comparison to help glean systematic lessons from sets of theoretically relevant historical episodes.

George sought ways of studying historical cases to draw out valid and policy-relevant lessons. A systematic understanding of the broader phenomena of which the cases were instances would aid policy makers in accurately diagnosing new cases of such phenomena. Policy makers could then make informed judgments about the choice of strategies and actions in new situations, despite the inherent uncertainty of international interactions.

Little was found at the time in the academic literature on methods for the rigorous and systematic study of historical experiences (George & Bennett, 2005). George and his colleagues set out to devise a case study methodology for conducting comparative analysis in ways that would connect analytical explanations of each case into a broader, more complex theory. This approach aimed to discourage subjective reliance on potentially flawed historical analogies but rather to identify specific causal patterns associated with the alternative outcomes that had resulted from using different strategies under varied sets of conditions.

In order "to analyze past instances of each of the generic problems to identify conditions and procedures that were associated with successful or failed outcomes" (George & Bennett, 2005, pp. x–xi), approaches were developed for converting historical and descriptive explanations of case conditions and outcomes into analytic explanations built from theory-driven variables. The outcome served as a dependent variable to be explained by the conditions analyzed as independent variables. This method did not intend or permit using the findings of a few cases that were not necessarily representative to estimate a probability distribution for the entire universe of instances of, for example, deterrence. Rather, the method enabled what George called "contingent generalizations" intended to help practitioners diagnose new situations and select or prescribe a solution strategy from among the available options, as medical practitioners might do in a clinical setting.

We return to one of Alexander George's structured-focused comparisons in Chapter 4, where we use his landmark study of coercive diplomacy as an example in providing the step-by-step instructions for calculating information metrics. At that same time, we demonstrate the ways in which the information method can enhance this prominent comparative case study.

Claude Shannon and a Mathematical Theory of Communication

Claude E. Shannon's fundamental insights that laid the groundwork for what became known as "information theory" also arose from the national security challenges of World War II and the Cold War. Shannon's work on intelligence ciphers for national defense brought him into contact with Alan Turing, who was in residence at the Bell Labs for two months in early 1943. Shannon conceptualized cryptography and other early computer science applications as instances of general problems of communication across noisy channels. The approach was formalized in his now famous 1948 paper on "A Mathematical Theory of Communication," published in *Bell System Technical Journal*. This paper argued that the fundamental problem of communication was that of "reproducing at one point either exactly or approximately a message selected at another point." The variation of meaning and other factors associated with each message could be systematically related to certain measurable physical or conceptual entities (much like independent variables). The central concern was to reduce uncertainty about the outcome (dependent variable) of a selection of an actual message from a set of possible messages and its delivery to destination intact (success) or not (failure). A systematic methodology had to be "designed to operate for each possible selection, not just the one which will actually be chosen since this is unknown at the time of design" (Shannon, 1948, p. 379). This methodology called for a universal perspective on the uncertainty and complexity of information, and that is what Shannon's information theory provided.

Shannon's conception of information had significant implications for a broad class of intelligence problems. Central questions revolved around how much information one needs to solve a particular problem, such as identifying the target and timing of an impending attack, to make an informed decision, such as what actions are needed to stop this attack. How much information is enough for a decision, and how do we know this decision is correct? These insights had practical implications for the collection and interpretation of information intercepted from secret, encrypted, or noisy signals intelligence channels or obtained from human intelligence sources. Intelligence collection is costly and puts people at risk. Questions such as how long to keep an agent in the field or intercept coded signals to decode a message accurately and timely could be decisive. Concrete measures to assess the magnitude of information needed and its uncertainty could constitute lifesaving and potentially strategic game-changing solutions.

In communication theory and engineering, these problems are particular instances of the general phenomenon of information transmission over noisy channels. In other words, how much do we know from the information we have? How much new information do we need to find out what we need to know, and how do we know? How do we assess the chances that this decision is correct? How do we systematically, unambiguously (quantitatively) measure the magnitude of uncertainty reduction or information gain from each new piece of data (such as a new message to be intercepted, new bits of transmission received, new case of a phenomenon to be observed and studied, new factors examined, etc.)? Shannon's information theory answered these questions.

From Cryptography and Communication to Comparative Case Studies

In the analysis of comparative case studies, we are seeking answers to essentially the same questions. Cases are conceptualized as instances of a more general phenomenon being studied. Given that we have the information obtained from the completed case studies—which relate some theorized explanatory factors (independent variables) to uncertain outcomes (dependent variables)—how much do we really know about the outcome, how much more do we learn from analyzing factors and comparing the cases, and how do we know whether we got it right? How do we systematically, unambiguously (quantitatively) measure the uncertainty reduction and the information gain contributed by each case study or by each variable about the uncertain outcome of a phenomenon of which the cases are selected instances?

Shannon's (1948) approach used the concept of "information entropy"—a measure of uncertainty and complexity he adapted from physics. Because the questions Shannon posed tackled fundamental problems of information, the answers had utility far beyond his original applications.

Our application extends the concept of information entropy further into the domain of knowledge gained from analyzing configurations of complex information. The challenge of drawing inferences from comparative case studies can be conceptualized as a problem of information and communication. Knowledge is obtained from information observed and systematically compared based on instances (cases) of a phenomenon. The central question is, *How much does the information contained in the explanatory factors across a set of cases reduce our uncertainty about the outcome of interest?* The same information uncertainty principles that Shannon developed apply.

Our systematic methodology builds on a synthesis of the analytic principles proposed by Alexander George in the structured-focused comparative case method and the rigorous and replicable metrics developed in Claude Shannon's information theory.

Making Qualitative Analysis of Information Systematic: The Method of Structured-Focused Comparison

We live in a world of both too little and too much information. Because there is too little information, we need a scientific approach to help us draw larger inferences from what little information we have. But there is also too much information, in that the world is full of irrelevant noise. This is particularly true in the modern era of big data and ubiquitous Internet access. Identifying useful information can be difficult when it is hidden among the vast quantities of data increasingly being recorded and streamed every second of every day. Identifying accurate information can also be challenging because it requires deeper knowledge and the ability to evaluate information. The solution to these problems is theory combined with appropriate research methods. We use theories to help us identify the outcomes we should be interested in and to identify the factors that might be connected to those outcomes. These theoretical elements allow us to develop hypotheses about the logic of those connections that can then be evaluated empirically.

The method of structured-focused comparison starts from theory. Theory allows us to pick out the most promising explanatory variables. This is particularly important for small-*n* comparative cases where, by definition, we do not have a lot of degrees of freedom. The method then provides a set of systematic guidelines and procedures for drawing valid inferences and making contingent generalizations as well as cumulating knowledge from comparative case studies.

George and Bennett (2005, pp. 6–7) articulate the method of structured-focused comparison within the broader framework of the role of case studies in theory development in the social sciences. The book codifies the best practices of case studies, clarifies their comparative advantages, and engages the relevant debates in the philosophy of science. The method of structured-focused comparison interacts with all aspects of theory development, from generation of new hypotheses to testing of existing ones. The method's particular strengths lie in engaging typological theories for modeling and explaining complex contingent generalizations. By systematically investigating factor-outcome relationships in different types of case and variable interactions, the method is designed to generate inferences capable of producing "generic knowledge" that policy makers can use. The results can help scholars and practitioners gauge new situations and develop effective strategies informed by theoretically guided empirical insights.

Structured-focused studies often draw together the contributions of many researchers by incorporating multiauthor cases selected explicitly into a common theory-driven design or by creating meta-analytic frameworks where different studies may be compared on relevant elements. These approaches make insights more comparable, which encourages the cumulation of findings from individual efforts into a larger ordered body of knowledge. Complementarities with information-theoretic approaches emerge from the shared focus on systematic and replicable procedures.

Structured-Focused Comparison: What Is It and How to Do It

The method of structured-focused comparison was developed to study historical experience in ways that would generate useful generic knowledge for important policy problems. The method enables drawing explanations of each case of a particular phenomenon into a broader, more complex theory. The systematic results can inform a better understanding of historical events and, most important, help diagnose and deal with possible new cases (George & Bennett, 2005, pp. 67–72).

The logic of structured-focused comparison is simple and straightforward. The method is "structured" around general research questions determined by the investigator to reflect the objectives of the study. Data collection is standardized and guided by asking the same questions of each case. The same replicable procedures are used to collect and analyze the data for each case. These provisions make systematic cross-case comparison and cumulation of the findings possible. The method is "focused" by dealing only with specific, theoretically determined aspects of the examined cases (George & Bennett, 2005, pp. 67–72).

The requirements for structure and focus apply not only to multicase studies but to single case studies as well. Carefully constructed single case studies will enable researchers to replicate the findings and to later join them with other cases in a comparative framework.

What is a "case" in such case studies? The structured-focused comparison method provides a universal definition: *A case is defined as an instance of a class of events* (George & Bennett, 2005, p. 17). The term *class of events* in this context refers to a phenomenon of interest, such as deterrence, coercive diplomacy, wars, peace treaties, terrorist attacks, educational programs, types of economic systems, political regimes, medical treatments, policy decisions, management actions, business startups, or other phenomena to be evaluated, theorized about, and explored though particular cases.

On the basis of the problem chosen for investigation, the researcher establishes the universe—that is, the specific class or subclass of events—from which the cases shall be selected as instances for theoretically driven study. The specific selection of one or several cases is guided by clearly defined research objectives and an appropriate research strategy to achieve that objective. We address the critical role of case selection in Chapter 3. Suffice it for now to emphasize that for valid scientific inference, it is insufficient and inappropriate to choose cases that are simply interesting or well endowed with available data. A logical rationale is required for how a case contributes to investigating some broader phenomenon, of which the chosen case is an instance. Finally, structured-focused case studies identify variables of theoretical interest for purposes of explanation, scientific inference potential, and leverage for policy makers or other practitioners to enable them to influence outcomes (George & Bennett, 2005, p. 69).

Now we can turn to how such case studies are done. We review several examples of structured-focused case studies in the later chapters in the context of our detailed and step-by-step demonstrations of the use of information metrics. The basic process for structured-focused case study is illustrated in Figure 1.1, which also emphasizes where information metrics fit to enhance the results.

As illustrated in Figure 1.1, the implementation process involves three phases, each with several specific tasks (adapted from George & Bennett, 2005, chap. 4–6):

- *Phase I: Theory and Research Design*. Research design tasks apply for all types of systematic, theory-oriented research. The tasks, which are interrelated and should fit together within an integrated design framework, include the following: (1) Specify the problem and research objective. (2) Develop a research strategy to achieve that objective, including specification of the dependent (outcome) variable to be explained or predicted and the independent and intervening variables (explanatory factors) to be explored within the study's theoretical framework. (3) Describe the way the variables vary.

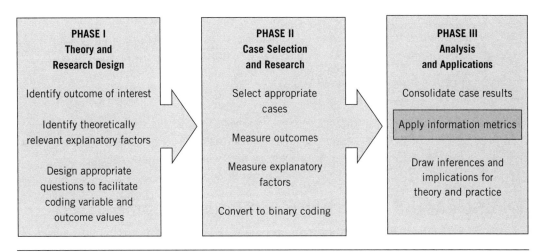

PHASE I Theory and Research Design	PHASE II Case Selection and Research	PHASE III Analysis and Applications
Identify outcome of interest	Select appropriate cases	Consolidate case results
Identify theoretically relevant explanatory factors	Measure outcomes	Apply information metrics
Design appropriate questions to facilitate coding variable and outcome values	Measure explanatory factors Convert to binary coding	Draw inferences and implications for theory and practice

Figure 1.1   The Structured-Focused Comparison Process Enhanced With Information-Theoretic Metrics

Although outcome variables may be classified or coded straightforwardly as success or failure, the underlying phenomenon thus measured may involve much complexity and variability. The researcher needs to understand and reflect this complexity in the coding and measures to maintain external and internal validity as well as replicability of the procedures for comparison and cumulative impact. (4) Formulate data requirements. These are the specific questions to ask of each of the cases (i.e., the questions around which the study is structured and focused) and the standardized procedures so each case study can be carried out replicably, comparably, and consistently with the overall design integrated across all these tasks.

- *Phase II: Case Selection and Research.* Select appropriate cases (Chapter 3 is dedicated to this critical task). The systematic "answers" to the specific research questions for each of the cases constitute the data for structured-focused comparison. The researcher devises provisional explanations and considers the problem of competing explanations and how the evidence can be used to sort out the most informative factors. Descriptive evidence is structured around illuminating the central uncertainties, and all evidence is assessed to develop analytical explanations.

- *Phase III: Analysis and Applications.* Case studies can have implications for theory and practice. Theory development and testing may involve drawing lessons learned or actionable insights for evaluating future cases or decisions. Case study findings may serve to establish, strengthen, or weaken existing explanations, and they may be generalized conditionally to the broader class of phenomena of which the cases are instances or, possibly, to related phenomena. For theory development, results may offer historical explanation, contingent generalization, and potentially generalization across types. For theory testing, the findings may be used to test competing explanations of cases, test contingent generalizations or the scope or domain of their application, or probe potential implications across types in a typological theory.

The details of these phases and tasks must be adapted to specific investigations, but they provide a set of guidelines rooted in the standards of the scientific method to make structured-focused comparisons qualitatively rigorous and systematic.

The Strengths of Structured-Focused Comparison

As with any scientific methodology, structured-focused comparison has its strengths and limitations. This systematic approach is more amenable to replication and cumulation, and it can be used to develop and assess theory as well as draw contingent generalizations for informing policy decisions.

In a broader methodological landscape, case studies tend to be strong where statistical methods and formal models tend to be weak, insufficient, or inapplicable. This is a basis for the increasingly accepted scholarly recognition of important complementarities in the value and use of alternative methods.

The advantages of structured-focused comparisons for testing hypotheses and developing theory include "their potential for achieving high conceptual validity; their strong procedures for fostering new hypotheses; their value as a useful means to closely examine the hypothesized role of causal mechanisms in the context of individual cases; and their capacity for addressing causal complexity" (George & Bennett, 2005, pp. 19–22).

The Limits of Structured-Focused Comparison

The critical limitation of traditional structured-focused comparisons is that the admirable qualitative rigor of their design and conduct still comes down to relying on subjective assessment of the results. The central problem of many comparative studies is a lack of systematic assessment in the presentation and analysis of cases. We have reviewed case studies across a number of fields and can report that apart from those studies disciplined by *qualitative case analysis* (QCA) methods, which we discuss in Chapter 7, this lack of a comprehensive overview is exceedingly common.

It is also important to note the recurrent trade-offs that are often necessitated by small-*n* research designs. These include trade-offs between the richness of detail and specific explanations of particular events and the parsimony of analytical explanations with inferential value beyond the immediate cases. Case authors must address the tension between achieving high internal validity for their particular explanations versus making analytical or contingent generalizations for broader classes of phenomena. These trade-offs are often shaped by case selection, as we examine more in depth in Chapter 3.

Finally, George and Bennett (2005) themselves point out limitations in the structured-focused comparison methodology, including a "relative inability to render judgments on the frequency or representativeness of particular cases and a weak capability for estimating the average 'causal effect' of variables for a sample. Potential limitations can include indeterminacy and lack of independence of cases" (p. 22).

Notably, George and Bennett (2005, p. 34) conclude their discussion of their method's limitations with an appeal to scholars to take advantage of the opportunities for multimethod research to correct for limitations and enhance the overall value of this and other methods in our scientific toolkit. Our information theory approach is one answer to this call.

Structured-Focused Comparison: The Bottom Line

As George and Bennett (2005) have argued, the techniques of structured-focused comparison effectively discipline the process of conducting case study analysis. The central limitation of this approach has been the lack of a systematic way to assess the results and frequently weak implementation that fails to build an overarching analytic picture.

We leverage the complementary use of information theory to make structured-focused comparison studies more systematic and rigorous. This approach also forces analysts to present their case study material methodically and to draw clear analytic conclusions. Information analytics are designed to counter the limitation of subjective eyeballing of results with concrete, systematic, and substantive measures that are easy to produce and use. While compensating where possible for case study shortcomings, the information metrics make the information value of results explicit. Most important, while contributing additional tools to enhance small-*n* analysis, this approach preserves the in-depth knowledge and nuance that are the traditional strength of comparative case study research.

Information Theory and Metrics for Qualitative Learning

The information connection for case study research arises from our interest in measuring how informative knowledge of an observed factor is about an outcome. That is, how much does knowing the value of a particular factor reduce our uncertainty about an outcome of interest? A well-established body of work in information theory provides a solid foundation for producing this kind of assessment in comparative case studies.

Mutual information is a comprehensive measure of uncertainty reduction that is suitable for identifying relationships among variables with the complex or unknown underlying probability distributions that are likely in small-n work. It is based on Shannon's information entropy measure, a universal measure of uncertainty of and complexity of information. Traditional statistical measures, such as those based on the central limit theorem or on other sampling dynamics, are not reliable for small numbers of observations. Mutual information is a more sensitive and accurate measure of interdependency among variables because it can uncover relationships not detected by measures based around a central tendency or other limited characteristics, such as correlation, variance, and so on.

The central question may be whether this is the right measure to use. The information metric has a number of advantages: It is not a constructed or sample-based estimate. It is simple to calculate and relatively robust. Because it is not parametric and is simply an expression of the information relationship between an outcome and an independent variable, it is difficult to go wrong in the interpretation of the metric itself. It does not depend on sample size for convergence. It makes no distributional assumptions. Mutual information applies exactly when we cannot verify or rely on such assumptions, as in the world of small-n case studies, about highly complex underlying phenomena. It is a precise understanding of the ability of the observed values of one variable to convey information about a second variable, as well as a precise measure of independence when mutual information is zero. The metric is based on an established body of information theory and has acknowledged benefits over other binary correspondence measures or quantitative tools (Brown, Cai, & DasGupta, 2001).

Of course, there are still dangers in making inferences from the case study results. Just as correlation is not causality, information is not causality. But these are the problems of any case study and stem from case selection and interpretation rather than from the information method. Analysts will draw inferences from small-n studies. Our argument is that they should do so guided by more concrete metrics rather than by relying only on subjective assessment. Providing a systematic and replicable measure can help make the results of small-n studies, including those conducted with QCA, much clearer.

The information metric is attractive conceptually and has comparative advantages that have been thoroughly explored. It is straightforward to calculate and, as we demonstrate in Appendix A, can be done simply in a spreadsheet. The primary mathematical requirement of the analyst is to do counting. If there are fewer than 10 cases, the fingers can be used.

A Road Map for Quantifying the Qualitative

In *Quantifying the Qualitative,* we walk you through the core information-theoretic techniques for the systematic analysis of comparative case studies. We start in Chapter 2 with an overview of information theory and the conceptual groundwork for its use in comparative case study. We also review the basic probability and mathematical concepts (simply based around multiplication and addition) that are used for calculating the information measures.

In Chapter 3, we examine the critical issues surrounding case selection. The information metrics that we develop provide a systematic and reproducible method for describing the relationship between a set of factors and an outcome variable. The ability to draw inferences from the cases to the broader world still depends on the quality of the cases and how they were chosen. One of the virtues of this method is that the metrics themselves are unaffected by case selection issues. They can be applied transparently to convenience samples or even to cherry-picked or biased sets of cases. But the ability to draw inferences from the case studies still relies on the analyst's awareness of case selection issues.

Chapter 4 is where we lay out the step-by-step details for calculating information metrics for comparative case study using a prominent example of a structured-focused study. We show how these measures are calculated from simple data counts and go over their interpretation and their use in communicating systematic analytic results from comparative case study.

In Chapter 5, we provide three diverse real-world examples of information metrics at work. We apply information metrics to reanalyze three published examples of comparative case studies, from the fields of ecology, education, and medicine, respectively. We show how information theory provides replicable metrics for understanding which factors communicate the most information about the outcome of interest. In each case, information theory allows us to draw more detailed and methodical conclusions about these case studies and identify important issues overlooked by subjective assessments alone.

Chapter 6 addresses the issue of sensitivity analysis and confidence intervals for information metrics. Because this approach generates reproducible and transparent quantitative indicators for the relationship between each factor and the outcome, we can easily assess the influence of different kinds of operationalization, measurement, and interpretation errors. We show systematically how dropping or recoding individual cases affects the information conditions. It is also possible to develop confidence intervals on these measures to account for some kinds of error, although we argue that these may be of relatively limited utility for small ns.

In Chapter 7, we discuss the relationship of information metrics to the widely used techniques of QCA. This is an approach for reducing the number of factors through the use of Boolean logic. We show that information metrics can be complementary to QCA and can help better understand the impact of the different reduced-form factors identified through QCA analysis.

Chapter 8 is the traditional conclusion. We review the strengths and limits of the information method for comparative case analysis and discuss some extensions. In particular, we consider the benefits of information metrics for policy makers and policy analysts. Because of its transparency and simplicity, our method can be of great use for the policy community where comparative program analysis is a regular requirement and where the number of cases and quantitative capabilities or interests of the relevant audiences may not allow for traditional statistical analysis or may render it of lesser value.

We have included two appendixes that demonstrate the use of Excel and the statistical software package R for facilitating and automating the calculation of information metrics.

Conclusion

Despite the ongoing revolution in big data, comparative case analysis remains a critical methodology across a broad range of fields. Our purpose in this book is to introduce a simple, systematic, and replicable metric for analyzing the impact of different explanatory variables on some outcomes of interest. This straightforward metric is simple to calculate ("If you can count, you can do it") and thus is accessible to researchers and policy makers with quite varying degrees of quantitative experience or aptitude. Interestingly, it arises from the same foundational work that made big data and the Information Age possible. That foundation is the primary subject of the next chapter.

Additional resources are provided at http://study.sagepub.com/drozdova.

The Information Revolution

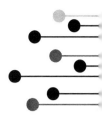

Information theory draws on the rich scientific and applied developments of the Information Revolution we discussed in Chapter 1. It also connects to basic concepts of probability, uncertainty, and complexity. In this chapter, we provide a deeper intellectual background for the relatively simple yet profound information analytics that we apply toward enhancing comparative case studies. We start with an overview of information theory and the conceptual groundwork for its use in comparative case study. We then introduce the information metrics and provide an intuitive review of the probability and mathematical concepts that facilitate their calculation. Finally, we highlight information theory's multifaceted contributions and some practical benefits of our method.

Information Theory for the Information Age

In Chapter 1, we set the stage for the origins of the Information Age and the developments in both information theory and systematic case study approaches. Both contributed better ways to learn about and survive in the complex new world. As action under uncertainty became more consequential, scholars and decision makers sought better analytic, technological, and practical ways to understand and handle uncertainty.

In the wake of the Second World War, after earning his PhD from MIT, Claude Shannon was working at Bell Labs, where he became involved in two military projects. One project focused on antiaircraft weapons and more generally on air defense. Fire control parameters had to be calculated from radar data, and the project presented a case of the more general problems of signal processing in the transmission, manipulation, and utilization of intelligence. In essence, it was a case of separating a signal from interfering noise in communication systems. The other project was in the field of cryptography—a different case of the same set of underlying fundamental problems of complex communications over noisy and uncertain channels (Segal, 2008, pp. 424–430). Wartime demanded ways to reduce that uncertainty. Shannon's insight was to focus not on transmission lines but rather on accurate and efficient communication of complex information despite the noise (Horgan, 1990, pp. 22–22B).

Prior to Shannon's path-breaking work, it was assumed that as the amount or complexity of information being transmitted increased, the probability of error went up. Shannon demonstrated that if we had a way to quantify the quality of information, we could design communication systems that could be essentially errorless. He further showed that the optimal way to quantify information was through *information entropy*. This insight became the foundation for his seminal article on the mathematics of communication and then, in turn, the basis for the digital revolution.

These exciting developments shape our interest in applying the notion of information entropy. It can help us enhance the communication of complex information in comparative case studies. Our application provides ways of gaining a clear and accurate understanding of *qualitative* signals collected in, or distorted by, uncertain and noisy environments of case study data.

What Is Entropy and Why Information Entropy

We will turn to our very straightforward approach to calculating relevant entropy metrics for case studies later in this chapter and in Chapter 4. Before we get there, it is helpful to look a little more at the origins and the meaning of these ideas—to understand why information metrics are the way they are and later use that intuition when we apply them to case studies. The intellectual heritage of the idea of entropy traces the scientific, technological, and economic leaps of civilization over the past couple of centuries and beyond. The original understanding of the concept of entropy came from advances in thermodynamics applied to make steam engines more efficient as they drove the Industrial Revolution. It would go on to tame the atom, unleash high-tech computing, and create cyberspace.

In thermodynamics, a branch of thermal physics, the concept of "entropy" may be understood as a measure of the number of ways (states) the components of a system can arrange themselves, while conforming to some set of constraints. "Thermal physics is the fruit of the union of statistical and mechanical principles. Mechanics tells us the meaning of work; thermal physics tells us the meaning of heat" (Kittel & Kroemer, 1980, p. 7). Statistics tells us the meaning of chance. Together, these foundations inform the fundamental premises entropy is designed to capture—namely, *the greater the number of possible states, the greater the complexity of the system* or, alternatively, *the more unknowable which state the system will be in, the greater our uncertainty about the system*. Entropy connects these notions to convey, respectively, how diverse the system is and how much we are lacking in its understanding.

The enduring power of entropy analysis comes from its ability to help us gain a great deal of quantitative insight into complex system behaviors based solely on *analyzing the overall predictability of the arrangement of its elements, without the need to follow the behavior of the individual elements themselves*. This great simplification helps not only when the number of elements is very large as is the case in physics settings, but especially—and most relevantly to the subject of our book—when the behavior of individual system components is complex or uncertain and the number of observations (cases) is small. Entropy analysis is effective and efficient. While it can be rigorously shown that all properties of an arbitrary system can be encapsulated in an appropriate probability distribution, for complex systems these tend to be very complicated (e.g., particle wave functions in quantum physics) and are usually unknown or very difficult to represent accurately. Thus, scientists and practitioners have sought more straightforward measures of uncertainty and complexity. It is possible to extract some cumulative quantity that will efficiently measure the most relevant properties of the probability distribution that describes the system in depth and detail. Entropy is that measure. *Entropy gives us a number—rather than a complicated function—to represent uncertainty, complexity, and information. Entropy measures are precise, rigorous, and useful.*

Having proved itself in the context of physics, the idea that by focusing on entropy one can gain profound quantitative insights into overall system structure and/or behavior—even from qualitative or limited knowledge of its individual components—was adopted into and further advanced across a number of other academic fields. In practical terms, the biggest breakthrough came with Shannon's application of entropy toward the understanding and optimization of information quantification, storage, and communication. In the original development of entropy analysis, physicists focused on deriving the entropy measures for only the most likely states of a system. This was the appropriate calculation for thermal physics, given the second law of thermodynamics (the law of increasing entropy; Kittel & Kroemer, 1980, chap. 2; Landau & Lifshitz, 1964, chaps. 7 and 8). As the notion of entropy was adapted into other fields, it became apparent that the analysis needed to include all possible states, rather than just the most likely. One of Shannon's central contributions in the development of information theory was to show how an "information entropy" measure could be formulated to take into account all possible states.

Over the past century—particularly, with the rise of quantum mechanics—physicists themselves have come to recognize information as the fundamental building block of the universe. It is interesting to note, for example, that one of the places where the most likely state approach proved inadequate was in astrophysics. Stephen Hawking (1976) and others used information theory for groundbreaking work on understanding the dynamics of black holes. Our cover illustration is a remarkable NASA image of a black hole swallowing a star, a phenomenon at the heart of significant academic work and controversy about what happens to information in these kinds of rare events. This implication applies to comparative case analysis as well. In particular, as we discuss in Chapter 3, case studies that include events of relatively low likelihood could still be of high theoretical or practical importance.

In his critical 1948 and subsequent papers, Shannon demonstrates that *any* information storage and communication can be thought of as an entropy problem as well. A textual message is a set of ordered letters. Holding aside punctuation, capitalization, and other possible symbols, each letter in a message can take on 26 possible values in the English alphabet. Letters must be represented as bits in order to be stored or communicated by modern computers. It takes one bit to distinguish between two possible states $\{0, 1\}$. It takes two bits to distinguish between four possible states ($2 \times 2 = 2^2$). Three bits can distinguish eight states ($2 \times 2 \times 2 = 2^3$). By five bits, we can distinguish $2^5 = 32$ states and thus could handle the lowercase alphabet. You can see that this calculation underlies the process of digital communication. You can thank Shannon every time you send a text message, listen to a digital music file, watch a streaming video, or make a transaction online.

Notice that in the preceding discussion, the number of states (q) that can be represented by n bits was equal to the power of 2, namely, $q = 2^n$. We have explicitly shown this for $q = 2, 4$, and 32 ($n = 1, 2$, and 5), but the formula can be shown to hold for any q. It follows that a way to quantify the increase in (computational) information complexity that comes with an increased number of system states is to invert the latter formula to find n in terms of q. That is, how many bits are required to represent any given piece of information? The resulting expression uses the logarithm in base 2, with the number of bits required to store q distinct symbols being $n = \log_2(q)$. (The "log" expression means the power to which we need to raise 2 to get q. We provide a tutorial on logarithms in the section on "What's Under the Hood" for those who could use a refresher. For now, think of it as a way to easily compute exponential relationships with a push of a button on a calculator or in Excel.)

This relatively simple notion is already very close to the concept of information entropy, which evolved from physics. Indeed, physical entropy is defined as the logarithm of the number of states accessible to the system (Kittel & Kroemer, 1980, p. 42). When the most likely state is sufficient, physical entropy is calculated using only the probability of the most likely state (p) by multiplying that probability by its log, $p \log p$. In other contexts, thinking about information entropy, we need to also take into consideration all possible states and that some states are more likely than others. As anyone who has played Scrabble knows, in an arbitrary collection of words, some letters appear much more often than others. To account for this, the information entropy formula will condition the logarithms by the different probabilities of the different letters and sum over all states. This sum expression is the average entropy over all states of the system. This is the intuition behind Shannon's information entropy formula.

Now we can see his formula and understand the reasoning. Shannon represented information communication as an uncertain process—more specifically, a type of probabilistic and evolving over time (stochastic) process, known as a Markov process, where future outcomes are estimated to be conditional only on present observations. He then sought to "define a quantity which will measure, in some sense, how much information is 'produced' by such a process, or better, at what rate information is produced? Suppose we have a set of possible events whose probabilities of occurrence are $p_1, p_2, \cdots, p_n$. These probabilities are known but that is all we know concerning which event will occur. Can we find a measure of how much 'choice' is involved in the selection of the event or of how uncertain we are of the outcome?" (Shannon, 1948, p. 392). Shannon labeled his information entropy measure with a symbol H, after similar formulations by the physicist Ludwig Boltzmann in his work on statistical mechanics and the second law of thermodynamics. Shannon's formula for information entropy should now make conceptual sense: It is a function of the probabilities of the possible states of a system, and it represents average entropy over all states:

$$H(p) = -\sum_{i=1}^{n} p_i \log_2 p_i$$

where n is a number of possible states; p_i is probability of each state, designated by a counter i ranging from 1 to n; the symbol Σ (Greek letter sigma) denotes summation across all states from 1 to n; and what is summed is the product of each state's probability and the logarithm (log) of that probability. Shannon's formula accounts for all uncertainty by summing over all the $p \log p$ terms. The log is base 2, so information entropy is measured in bits. The minus sign offsets the log being negative for the numbers in the $0 < p < 1$ range.

From this basic information entropy equation, we can also formulate the entropy of a specific binary variable. If X is a probabilistic variable, we can write $H(X)$ as its entropy:

$$H(X) = -\sum_{i=1}^{n} p_i(x) \log_2 p_i(x)$$

We will simplify this formula later and demonstrate in Chapter 4 how it can be easily used for handling small-n case study variables and qualitative data. Fundamentally, information entropy captures the essential (irreducible) computational complexity characteristic of any qualitatively describable system or, alternatively, the minimal amount of digital information necessary to accurately describe it to gain its detailed understanding. This property makes the information entropy framework particularly efficient and uniquely well suited for problems faced by qualitative scholars. Now we can understand uncertainty and complexity as two sides of the same coin—information entropy—the coin of the information realm.

Information in Case Studies

The goal in comparative case studies is to assess the relative contributions of a set of explanatory factors to communicating information about some outcome of interest. In setting out his mathematical approach to understanding communication, Shannon referenced R. C. Tolman's (1938/1979) *Principles of Statistical Mechanics,* where we find an interpretation of entropy that echoes our approach of communicating knowledge from case studies. Tolman states that the "entropy of a system is a measure of the degree of our ignorance as to its condition" (1938/1979, p. 561). We want to reduce that ignorance through measured information gain (entropy decrease) from observations. Measuring how much the explanatory factors in our case studies decrease the information entropy of a dependent variable provides a systematic basis for small-n analysis.

We know that this may seem like more math than you signed up for under the "if you can count, you can do it" plan. You'll have to trust us that this background material is just that, background material.

In Chapter 4, we work through our information-theoretic method step by step, and counting is all that will be required. Indeed, we can already offer one significant simplification of the information entropy metric. When we apply these methods to comparative case studies, we restrict the factors and outcomes to binary {0, 1} variables. (In Chapter 3, we discuss the binary coding approach for qualitative data, and in Chapter 8, we also comment on extensions of our method to account for multiple possible outcomes by scaling the basic binary approach.) From basic principles of probability, which we will review in more detail shortly, we also know that, with only two possible mutually exclusive outcomes, the probability of one of these alternatives equals 1 minus the probability of the other $(1 - p)$. The total probability adds up to the number 1, meaning that, with complete certainty, one or the other outcome will occur. With binary outcomes, the possible states are reduced to just two, and the entropy formula is simply:

$$H(X) = - p(x = 1) \log_2 (x = 1) - p(x = 0) \log_2 (x = 0)$$

The entropy of such a binary outcome is represented graphically in Figure 2.1.

Figure 2.1 helps us observe the properties of H, which substantiate it as an intuitive as well as reasonable measure of uncertainty. $H = 0$ if and only if the probability of a particular outcome is either 0 or 1. That is, when we are certain of the outcome—one way or the other—the uncertainty disappears, and the measure of uncertainty is zero. Otherwise, H is positive, meaning that at least some uncertainty exists. H is maximum when the probabilities of the possible outcomes are equal. In the binary case, this means a 50/50 chance, which accords intuitively with the most uncertain situation.

Thus far, we have looked at an entropy score for a single variable. In the binary case, $H(Y)$ tells us our total uncertainty about whether Y is 0 or 1, based on the probability, p, that Y is 1. For the purposes of comparative case study, however, it is critical to see that information entropy also equips us with a way to measure the uncertainty of Y given some other available knowledge about another variable, X, believed or theorized to be somehow associated with Y. In our case study language, X would be an independent variable based on which we would seek to reduce uncertainty about a dependent variable Y. In a typical case study research design, there are likely to be several Xs.

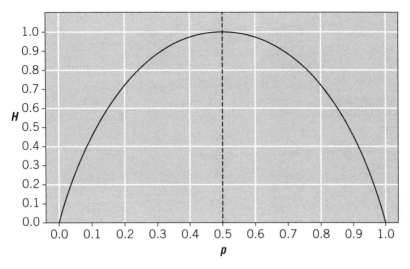

A graph of Information Entropy H, *measured in bits, in the case of two alternative outcome possibilities with probabilities* p *and* (1 − p).

Figure 2.1   Information Entropy of a Binary Outcome

Information theory gives us precise and insightful ways to address these analytical challenges. The approach relies on some very basic notions of logarithms and probability—including total, joint, and conditional probability—to establish more complex uncertainty measures. Before introducing these measures, we provide a brief primer on a few aspects of logarithms and probability concepts to ensure that our method is fully accessible to all readers. (Readers who are well versed in this material may skip ahead to the section titled "Information Uncertainty Measures.")

What's Under the Hood: A Primer on Logarithms and Probability for Small-*n* Analysis

Since it is our goal to make the information theory approach to comparative case analysis available to a wide range of scholars and practitioners, we briefly review this basic mathematical foundation. For those with even a minimal math background, this will all be quite elementary.

The Log Transformation

An intuitive understanding of logarithms usually starts with the simpler understanding of exponential functions. Exponentiation indicates how many times a number should be multiplied by itself. 5^2 is just 5×5. Similarly, 5^3 is $5 \times 5 \times 5$ and so on.

The logarithm is the inverse of an exponential function. Formally, the logarithm of a is the value of the exponent to which a base number must be raised to produce a. The general form $y = \log_b a$ reads "y equals log of a base b" and means that $b^y = a$, assuming $b > 0$. If $a = 16$, then $\log_4 (16) = 2$ since 4 has to be squared to get 16. In base 2, 16 would be written as $\log_2 (16) = 4$, since 16 is 2^4. (You may wonder what happens if $a = 0$. This special situation is discussed in a Technical Note at the very end of this Chapter.)

While your first response may be incredulity that anyone would wish to make such a transformation, the logarithm has proven exceedingly useful. The basic magic of logarithms is that they can solve difficult multiplication and division problems by turning them into simple addition or subtraction problems: $\log_b (x \times y) = \log_b (x) + \log_b (y)$. This shift was the basis of the slide rule, which enabled scientists to quickly solve intimidating calculations in that dark time before the advent of the four-function calculator.

You can easily calculate $\log_2$ with any spreadsheet program. In Microsoft Excel or Google Sheets, the function is $=\log(a, 2)$. If your phone's scientific calculator only has a $\log_{10}$ function, you can get the base 2 log of a by entering $\log_{10} (a)/\log_{10} (2)$.

Scientists preferred the intuitive notion of addition for understanding what happens to the total uncertainty of a system when you combine the uncertainty of its components.
If there are two independent random variables and the first has A possible outcomes, while the second has B possible outcomes, the uncertainty from the two variables together is multiplicative: A times B. This becomes more mathematically tractable and better fits the intuition that uncertainty should be additive, if we express it in logarithms, so that the joint uncertainty of A and B can be expressed by $\log (A) + \log (B)$ possible combinations.

Why Probability

The information metrics we advance here are tied to several core notions about probability. While, of course, entire books have been written about probability, the probability concepts we need to use here are very straightforward and relatively intuitive. As we demonstrate in Chapter 4, our information metrics can be calculated from simple counting. They can be easily done by hand or with an automated spreadsheet program such as Excel or a statistical program such as R, as we demonstrate in the Appendixes.

The counting process can be seen as reflecting the *relative frequency approach* to calculating and interpreting probability (Hogg & Craig, 1995, chap. 1). Our empirical approach to information theory is based on the patterns of co-occurrence in straightforward binary {0, 1} variables. It does not require the user to be proficient in probability theory, which can become philosophically and mathematically more challenging in a very small-n environment. Nonetheless, simple probability concepts are useful for describing the patterns of co-occurrence that drive our approach, including the joint, total, and conditional probability, which we take up in turn.

In each case, we begin with a 2 × 2 table showing all of the possible combinations of X and Y values. For convenience, we will label these four cells *ABCD*, using uppercase letters when the cells contain counts, as shown in Table 2.1.

For the purposes of illustration, we can start with a data set with 10 observations distributed so that the number in each cell is as shown in Table 2.2.

Joint Probability

For our purposes, we are interested in the probability that any selected independent variable takes on a specific value at the same time that the dependent variable takes on a specific value. That is, over the whole set of cases, how often is it that a given pattern occurs between the dependent variable and one of the independent variables? These values can be determined with simple counts. Count the number of times the pattern occurs and then divide by a count of the total number of possible combinations. Since we are working with binary values (True/False represented by 1 and 0, respectively), there are exactly four possible permutations for any combination of an X variable and the Y variable, as represented in the four cells of Table 2.1 and 2.2.

The joint probability of any particular one of these combinations is the number of times that combination occurs divided by the total number of cases ($n = 10$ in our example). Using the notation from Table 2.1, the four joint probabilities are *A/n, B/n, C/n,* and *D/n.* If we have the 10 cases illustrated in Table 2.2, where there are 3 cases in which X and Y are both present, then the joint probability is $3/10 = 0.3$. Table 2.3 shows the calculation of joint probabilities for the example distribution from Table 2.2. Each joint probability represents the proportion of all cases that fall in each cell. We will label these joint probability values with the lowercase letters *abcd* and will be using them in future calculations.

Total Probability

The total probability of a particular event accords with our intuitive notion of the likelihood of an event measured on

Table 2.1 Counting the X and Y Value Combinations

	X = 1	X = 0
Y = 1	A	B
Y = 0	C	D

Table 2.2 Counts of X and Y Value Combinations

	X = 1	X = 0
Y = 1	3	4
Y = 0	1	2

Table 2.3 Joint Probabilities

	X = 1	X = 0
Y = 1	a = 0.3	b = 0.4
Y = 0	c = 0.1	d = 0.2

Joint probability of (Y = 1 and X = 1):
$$a = 3/10 = 0.3$$
Joint probability of (Y = 1 and X = 0):
$$b = 4/10 = 0.4$$
Joint probability of (Y = 0 and X = 1):
$$c = 1/10 = 0.1$$
Joint probability of (Y = 0 and X = 0):
$$d = 2/10 = 0.2$$

Table 2.4   Total Probabilities

		$X = 1$	$X = 0$	**Total Probabilities for Y**
	$Y = 1$	$a = 0.3$	$b = 0.4$	0.7
	$Y = 0$	$c = 0.1$	$d = 0.2$	0.3
Total Probabilities for X		0.4	0.6	

Total probability of $(Y = 1)$: $(a + b) = 0.3 + 0.4 = 0.7$
Total probability of $(X = 1)$: $(a + c) = 0.3 + 0.1 = 0.4$
Total probability of $(Y = 0)$: $(c + d) = 0.1 + 0.2 = 0.3$
Total probability of $(X = 0)$: $(b + d) = 0.4 + 0.2 = 0.6$

a [0, 1] scale, meaning the range from 0 to 1, inclusively. If the probability is 0, there is no chance of the event occurring. If the probability is 1, the event is certain. We calculate this probability from the number of times the event occurs divided by the total number of cases. So, if our independent variable X is measuring whether a case subject is male or female, and there are 7 males and 3 females in our 10 cases, then the total probability of being male is $7/10 = 0.7$, and the total probability of being female is $3/10 = 0.3$.

You can also see that deriving the total probability of X requires adding together the cases when $X = 1$ and $Y = 0$ and the cases when $X = 1$ and $Y = 1$. The total probability that $X = 1$ comes from adding up all of the counts in the left-hand column of Table 2.2, where $X = 1$ and dividing that sum by n. The total probability that $X = 0$ comes from adding up all of the values in the right-hand column of Table 2.2, where $X = 0$ and dividing by n. The total probability that $Y = 1$ comes from adding up all of the counts in the top row where $Y = 1$ and dividing by n. The total probability that $Y = 0$ comes from adding up all of the counts in the bottom row where $Y = 0$ and dividing by n.

If you already have the *abcd* table with the joint probabilities in each cell, you can just add up the proportions. The total probability that $X = 1$ is the sum of the joint probabilities that $X = 1$ when $Y = 1$ and that $X = 1$ when $Y = 0$. Table 2.4 shows the derivation of the total probabilities. In this synthetic example, there are 10 cases, of which 7 are successes ($Y = 1$) and 3 are failures ($Y = 0$). The co-occurrences with successful ($X = 1$) and unsuccessful ($X = 0$) values for X are indicated by the numbers in the second row.

Conditional Probability

Conditional probability is the probability that the dependent variable takes on a specific value given that we already know the value of an independent variable. We notate this with a vertical separator line, $(Y|X)$. The conditional probability that a dependent variable Y takes the

Table 2.5 Conditional Probabilities

		$X = 1$	$X = 0$
	$Y = 1$	$a = 0.3$	$b = 0.4$
	$Y = 0$	$c = 0.1$	$d = 0.2$
Conditional probability that $Y = 1$ given value of X in column		0.75	0.67
Conditional probability that $Y = 0$ given value of X in column		0.25	0.33

Conditional probability of $(Y = 1 \mid X = 1)$: $a/(a + c) = 0.3/0.4 = 0.75$
Conditional probability of $(Y = 1 \mid X = 0)$: $b/(b + d) = 0.4/0.6 = 0.67$
Conditional probability of $(Y = 0 \mid X = 1)$: $c/(a + c) = 0.1/0.4 = 0.25$
Conditional probability of $(Y = 0 \mid X = 0)$: $d/(b + d) = 0.2/0.6 = 0.33$

value of 1 given that an independent variable X takes the value of 1 is notated $p(Y = 1 \mid X = 1)$. Again, all it takes is counting. Intuitively, the conditional probability is how many times Y takes on a specific value in those cases where X has taken a specific value. In our present example, we would isolate the cases where $X = 1$ and then count how many times $Y = 1$ among those. The conditional probability that $Y = 1$ given $X = 1$ would be the count of the cases where $Y = 1$ and $X = 1$ divided by the count of the number of cases where $X = 1$.

Once again, you can do these either from the raw counts (the *ABCD* values as in Tables 2.1 and 2.2) or directly from the joint probabilities (the *abcd* values as in Table 2.3). Table 2.5 shows the conditional probabilities for the same numeric example as in the previous Tables 2.2, 2.3, and 2.4.

We will use these probability concepts to calculate the information uncertainty measures and the case study metrics based on them. To fully establish our conceptual grounding, we can now return in a little more depth to Shannon's seminal contributions for understanding and harnessing the relationship between uncertainty and information.

Information Uncertainty Measures
· ·

We now have all the necessary background to introduce the remaining information concepts and formulas, which we will apply in the rest of the book to enhance comparative case study analytics. There are three interrelated core measures. First, *information entropy* measures the total uncertainty about an outcome (a dependent variable) in the absence of additional information about any possible explanatory factors (independent variables). Second, *conditional information entropy* measures the uncertainty about the outcome given that we know something about the presence or the absence of such factors. Third, *mutual information* ultimately measures what we have learned from observing such factors and what factors are more informative about the outcome in question. In terms of probability, mutual information is the amount of information one random variable contains about another, and in our comparative case study terms, this is the amount of information each independent variable contains about the dependent variable examined through a set of cases.

In addition to these three core information measures, we will also include a simple measure of *direction* to tell us whether the relationship between X and Y is positive or negative. That is, when X is present ($X = 1$), is Y more likely to be 1, a positive relationship, or 0, a negative relationship?

Information Entropy

Information entropy, in short, is the degree of uncertainty associated with a variable. Uncertainty tends to increase with complexity. To keep our conceptions and calculations more manageable, and in line with the substantive reasons already discussed, we are going to limit ourselves to binary variables, that is, variables that can only take the values of 0 or 1. We can think of these as variables capturing measures such as true/false, presence/absence, or success/failure.

The notions of total, joint, and conditional probability apply to assessing the information entropy of combinations of variables. Suppose there are two chance variables, X and Y, not necessarily statistically independent of one another. We will call Y an outcome variable, and X will represent a factor potentially affecting, explaining, or predicting the outcome—a factor we would potentially want to know about to reduce uncertainty about Y. Shannon's measure of information entropy (total uncertainty of a single variable) in the binary case is built from simple probability measures and the base 2 log of those probability measures:

$$H(Y) = -p(y = 1) \log_2 p(y = 1) - p(y = 0) \log_2 p(y = 0)$$

Since in the binary case, the probabilities that $y = 0$ and that $y = 1$ are complementary (i.e., they sum to 1), $p(y = 0) = 1 - p(y = 1)$. We can therefore rewrite $H(Y)$ entirely in terms of $p(y = 1)$:

$$H(Y) = -p(y = 1) \log_2 p(y = 1) - (1 - p(y = 1)) \log_2 (1 - p(y = 1))$$

We can also represent this in terms of the *abcd* joint probability values we used in Tables 2.3 to 2.5:

$$H(Y) = -(a + b) \log_2 (a + b) - (c + d) \log_2 (c + d)$$

All of this slightly fancy algebra leads to the smooth single peaked concave curve running from 0 to 1 and back to 0 as we saw in Figure 2.1. Such a curve is the intuitively appropriate shape for an information function. In the middle of the curve, where the probability of $Y = 1$ is close to 0.5, we have the greatest uncertainty about Y. When the probability of $Y = 1$ is exactly 0.5, we have no information that can help us know the value of Y, so information entropy is at its maximal value of 1. At each end of the curve, where the probability of $Y = 1$ is either 0 or 1, Y is perfectly predictable, so information entropy is 0.

Conditional Information Entropy

Information entropy tells us the amount of total uncertainty about a single variable such as our outcome Y in the absence of any additional information. Our real goal here, though, is to understand the relationship between an explanatory factor and an outcome variable. In terms of information, that means measuring how knowledge of the value of a factor (X) reduces our uncertainty about the dependent variable (Y). To build up to this measure of mutual information, we first need to calculate a measure of conditional information entropy, $H(Y|X)$. This intermediate measure allows us to systematically evaluate the level of uncertainty in Y given that we know whether the factor is present ($X = 1$) or not ($X = 0$). When several X factors are considered, we use the notation x_i:

$$H(Y = y \mid X = x_i) = -p(x_i = 0)\ [p(y = 0 \mid x_i = 0)\ \log_2 p(y = 0 \mid x_i = 0)$$
$$+ p(y = 1 \mid x_i = 0)\ \log_2 p(y = 1 \mid x_i = 0)]$$
$$- p(x_i = 1)\ [p(y = 0 \mid x_i = 1)\ \log_2 p(y = 0 \mid x_i = 1)$$
$$+ p(y = 1 \mid x_i = 1)\ \log_2 p(y = 1 \mid x_i = 1)]$$

The underlying conditional and joint probabilities are calculated based on simple counts as we already reviewed and then plugged into this equation to compute the conditional entropy. We provide more hands-on explanations and ample examples in Chapters 4 and 5.

We can also represent the conditional entropy metric a little more simply in terms of the *abcd* values used in Tables 2.3 through 2.5.

$$H(Y|X) = -(b + d)\ [(d/(b + d))\ \log_2 (d/(b + d))$$
$$+ (b/(b + d))\ \log_2 (b/(b + d))]$$
$$- (a + c)\ [(c/(a + c))\ \log_2 (c/(a + c))$$
$$+ (a/(a + c))\ \log_2 (a/(a + c))]$$

Arranging terms this can be further simplified to

$$H(Y|X) = -[d\ (\log_2 (d) - \log_2 (b + d)) + b\ (\log_2 (b) - \log_2 (b + d))]$$
$$- [c\ (\log_2 (c) - \log_2 (a + c)) + a\ (\log_2 (a) - \log_2 (a + c))]$$

Mutual Information

Mutual information tells us how much we can learn about Y from knowing X. It allows us to objectively, quantitatively measure the relative value of having knowledge about each of the different X variables. Mutual information measures the reduced uncertainty in Y due to the knowledge of X, written $I(Y; X)$. In other words, it measures information gain. Mutual information means the difference between the total entropy of Y and the uncertainty about the outcome given that we know whether a factor X is present or not. Mutual information is the difference between total and conditional uncertainty:

$$I(Y; X) = H(Y) - H(Y|X)$$
$$= I(Y = y; X = x_i)$$
$$= H(Y = y) - H(Y = y \mid X = x_i)$$

Conceptually, we show in the following chapters that it is easy to think about the numbers that result from these calculations as simple metrics of the degree to which knowledge of the value of X can tell us about the value of Y for the particular set of comparative cases under analysis.

Another way to think about this is in terms of the reduction in uncertainty about Y that comes from knowing about X. *The measures of information entropy, conditional information entropy, and mutual information are, respectively, the measures of total, conditional, and reduced uncertainty.* Intuitively, if the conditional entropy $H(Y|X)$ due to the knowledge of X is still large relative to the original total entropy $H(Y)$ alone, then the difference between them will be small, and mutual information $I(X; Y)$ gain will be small. However, if conditional entropy due to the knowledge of X is large, this difference will be large, indicating a relatively large mutual information gain from knowing X. *The higher the mutual information, the more valuable the knowledge gained from knowing X.*

Direction

Finally, it is important to include a measure that tells us whether the relationship between X and Y is positive or negative. The relationship is positive if the presence of X makes the presence of Y more likely. It is negative if the presence of X makes the presence of Y less likely. The direction of the relationship is often obvious from visual inspection, but this is not always so, especially when there are many cases or variables. Our measure for direction is derived simply from the diagonals of a 2 × 2 table. If there are more cases that fall in the main diagonal, where X and Y take on the same values, than in the off-diagonal, where X and Y take different values, then the direction is positive. Otherwise, it is negative.

In Table 2.6, we indicate the cell counts, again, with the *ABCD* notation and then show the calculation for *Direction* using those values.

The direction of the relationship is calculated by subtracting the off-diagonal values from the main diagonal values. If this number is greater than zero, then the relationship is positive. If it is less than zero, then the relationship is negative.

Table 2.6 The Direction Metric

	$X = 1$	$X = 0$
$Y = 1$	A	B
$Y = 0$	C	D

$$Direction = (A + D) - (B + C)$$

Direction can also be calculated from the joint probabilities (the *abcd* values) in the same way.

We will return to all of the information calculations in greater detail in Chapter 4. In that chapter and in Chapter 5, we provide several examples from different fields to demonstrate how simply and effectively the mutual information metric can enhance comparative case studies.

As Shannon (1948) specified in his original formulation of information theory, the uncertainty of *Y* is never increased by the knowledge of *X*s. The uncertainty of *Y* decreases due to knowledge of *X* or remains unchanged if *X* and *Y* are independent (*X* is uninformative about *Y*). Conditional entropy and mutual information can be calculated in more complex ways based on a variety of conditions modeled by combinations of several independent variables at a time as well as in terms of sequences of variables or other combinatorics. In this book, the initial binary combinations suffice for our purposes of introduction, and so as not to unduly overdetermine the small-*n* analysis. Nonetheless, the grasp of the foundations presented here fully enables a more advanced user to scale the metrics and apply the techniques in more complex ways.

Fundamental Contributions of Information Theory

Shannon's theory offered a unifying view of data and information with rigorous metrics applicable across a great variety of fields and problems. His fundamental contributions provided the following:

- *A universal view of data:* Shannon's particular application at the time was to data security, cryptography, and transmission of information in the form of 1s and 0s in computer science, but the approach could be used to represent different kinds of data, including qualitative data of comparative case studies as we will show.

- *Quantitative measures for representing information content of the data:* Information entropy–based measures provide objective and comparable metrics for ascertaining how much information is really contained or gained; these measures are universal and applicable to transmitting different sorts of information across a variety of channels and context environments.

Shannon's information theory solved two key challenges at the time: (1) how to extract information from data (especially from noisy or incomplete data such as those that are ciphered or affected by noisy transmission channels) and (2) how to represent complex information most efficiently when data could be represented and contained in different ways. This insight was fundamental to the efficient compression and transmission of data necessary for the Information Age, and continues to be ever more relevant to the modern era of big data.

Information theory is a widely used approach because it solves the nontrivial challenges of how much meaningful information a particular set of data contains and how to accurately and efficiently convey the intended information. The underlying complexities could be great, but information metrics give a concrete and meaningful summary number.

In Shannon's original formulation, information entropy is the minimum descriptive complexity of a random variable, and mutual information reflects the communication rate in the presence of noise. The noise may be completely meaningless and unrelated to a sought signal or contain the signal in some superfluously obscured way. We want to know if a signal is present and, if so, how to extract and best communicate it. Addressing fundamental questions in communication theory, Shannon's information theory answered what is the ultimate data compression (the entropy) and what is the ultimate transmission rate of communication (the channel capacity).

A communication channel is a system in which the output depends probabilistically on its input. Entropy in this context is a measure of the average uncertainty in the random variable, or the number of bits required on average to describe the random variable. Mutual information is a measure of the dependence between the two random variables. It is always nonnegative, and it is symmetric in X and Y. When mutual information is zero, the variables are independent. This central and broadly applicable insight offers a way to determine the relative magnitude of information that an observed independent variable, X, contains about the uncertain outcome states of a dependent variable, Y.

In their landmark text, *Elements of Information Theory*, Thomas Cover and Joy Thomas (2006) emphasize the advantage of information theory whereby mastering a few key ideas and techniques makes the subject "appear simple and provide great intuition on new questions"

(p. vxii). Among the simplicities inherent in information theory, they point out that, first, entropy and mutual information arise as the answers to fundamental questions, and, second, the answers to information-theoretic questions have a natural algebraic structure. Both features admit accessible, extensive applications and interpretations.

Reflecting on the impact of information theory across many fields since its inception, Cover and Thomas (2006) stressed the capability of information metrics to illuminate the entire problem being studied by the inspection of the answers: "Perhaps the outstanding examples of this in physics are Newton's laws and Schrödinger's wave equation. Who could have foreseen the awesome philosophical interpretations of Schrödinger's wave equation?" (p. vxii). Among other things, it ushered a fundamental understanding of quantum physics and posed new questions about uncertainty (see, e.g., Schrödinger, 1935/1980), which information theory has solved. One implication for our interest in applying information theory to case study research is that Schrödinger's wave function equation can be interpreted generically to say that outcomes are uncertain. However, once specific properties of the system are measured, the outcomes can become binary. This notion is conceptually similar to Alexander George's dichotomous vision of case outcomes, successful or failed, and the explicitly binary measures of case study variables for information analytics that we apply and explain more hands-on in Chapters 3 and 4.

The Growing Use of Information Metrics

Although Shannon's original development of information theory was motivated by fundamental problems of communication theory, data compression, and noisy channels, information science has evolved into a broader coherent field with diverse applications and growing use.

Information theory is a well-established subfield of applied mathematics. While ours is the first systematic treatment of the use of information theory as an analytic tool for enhancing comparative case analysis, information theory has been productively used in a number of other contexts across a variety of fields. Shannon's insights have made fundamental contributions to statistical physics in areas of thermodynamics, computer science in areas such as Kolmogorov complexity, and the class of statistical inference issues that have formalized the epistemological criterion known as Occam's razor (Cover & Thomas, 2006, chap. 1).

In addition to its initial applications in communications and its foundational role in computer science, information theory has provided leverage for a surprisingly wide range of more concrete problems.

Oil exploration has been facilitated by the use of information theory to distinguish between noise and relevant signals from seismic exploration tools and in designing optimal exploration patterns (Bickel & Smith, 2006; Minerbo, 1979). Information theory has helped us understand the ways in which DNA encodes living structures, and an entire field of biology— bioinformatics—has arisen to study the diverse ways in which information is stored and communicated in biochemical systems with nanotechnology and other applications (Hogeweg, 2011; Ramakrishnan & Bose, 2012; Samoilov, Arkin, & Ross, 2001). In physics, where information, and specifically the concept of entropy, was connected to thermodynamics, quantum theory and some of its core concepts, such as quantum entanglement and quantum complexity, have been built around information theory (Nielsen & Chuang, 2000). It has been used in finance to evaluate portfolios (Cover, 1991) and in data science for business (Provost & Fawcett, 2013).

Information theory has made similar inroads into the social sciences. Sociology, which has a longstanding interest in communication generally, has incorporated information dynamics into understanding networks and organizational structures (Bailey, 1994). Political and information scientists have used information theory to examine terrorist networks and political communication and to understand the characteristics of political systems (Drozdova & Samoilov, 2010; Sheingate, 2006). Information theory has contributed to the field of economics, where information is critical to the functioning of markets and can itself be a commodity (Arrow, 1996).

Information theory has been used to push boundaries across many domains. Improving comparative case analysis presents a similarly important and appropriate application. The good news is that, unlike most of these other areas, the technical requirements for understanding and sharing in the benefits of our use of information theory are dramatically lower. To set the stage for an information-theoretic approach to comparative case study, we really need only two relatively straightforward mathematical concepts: logarithmic transformations and basic probability based on simple counting as we explained in this chapter and demonstrate hands-on in Chapter 4.

A Note for Practitioners: From Analytics to Action

Alexander George's work on structured-focused comparisons, as we highlighted in Chapter 1, was a direct response to the dangers of the nuclear age and the analytic challenges of deterrence and more broadly war and peace (see, e.g., Acher & Snidal, 1989; Aleksandrov, 2002; Holloway, 1983; May, 1985). Scientific and technological developments alone, however, cannot spare human decision makers from the difficulty of making good judgments under uncertainty. Psychologists Amos Tversky and Daniel Kahneman (1974), in their landmark article, "Judgment Under Uncertainty: Heuristics and Biases," demonstrated empirically the many ways in which people, even experts, tend to exhibit mistaken judgment, misconstrue chances, rely on inaccurate subjective estimates of probability, form beliefs based on data of limited validity, and fall prey to faulty heuristics. This work has since advanced in many fields, but the challenges of human judgment remain (see, e.g., Radner, 2000). Information theory cannot solve all of these problems, but it offers concrete analytical tools to counter the risks of faulty judgment based on merely eyeballing case study results and then intuiting their meaning.

In addition to significantly enhancing the comparative case work of scholars, our information-theoretic approach can provide a useful tool for analysts, strategists, and policy makers. In a world that increasingly demands evidence-based justification for policy choices, our information metrics can help policy makers systematically sort through a thicket of data about initiatives and outcomes. It provides a straightforward and accessible approach both to conducting comparative evaluation of options and to communicating those results to a broad audience.

Policy makers and other practitioners have to make consequential choices under conditions of uncertainty. They often have to work with limited access to larger data sets or lack the quantitative skills to make effective use of them. Likewise, they usually need to communicate their findings to other decision makers or even to a public that will be challenged by the requirements or limitations for some nuanced problems of large-N statistics. Under these conditions, information metrics can be used to identify factors that most closely correspond to desired outcomes and can best inform the decisions.

For practitioners, as for scholars, the starting point is identifying the central factors that are believed to have an impact on the outcome of interest. Policy makers will be particularly interested in those factors that can be affected through policy initiatives but will also need to know about the relative importance of effects that are beyond their control.

It is also essential that practitioners exercise care in selecting the cases to study, an issue to which we return at greater length in Chapter 3. We particularly highlight the importance of understanding both success and failure cases together in a comparative perspective. It is sometimes tempting to only revel in successes or to ponder the failures alone, that is, to focus on only one type of outcome. To learn what factors may distinguish success from failure, however, we must evaluate a balanced mix of outcomes and factors toward identifying actionable lessons. We address this through research design and case selection as well as information metrics.

Conclusion

Information is the currency of our modern era. The work by Claude Shannon and others has helped articulate a more systematic way to understand and measure information. In this book, we focus on a particular kind of information: the information contained in well-structured case studies about particular outcomes of interest. Our argument is that this straightforward and accessible approach can help researchers as well as policy makers and other practitioners who are interested in moving beyond subjective assessment.

In addition to introducing the basic concepts of Shannon's groundbreaking approach to information, in this chapter, we have also set out the small set of mathematical concepts—some elements of probability and logarithms—that are required for our approach to quantifying qualitative case studies.

Before we turn our focus to the process of calculating information metrics, we must take a little time to discuss the critical issue of case selection. While the calculation of our information metrics for comparative case study analysis is relatively impervious to case selection issues, the ability to draw inferences from case studies is fundamentally tied to the quality of case selection. It is imperative, then, to review these important issues before we turn, in Chapter 4, to the step-by-step instructions for calculating systematic and replicable comparative case metrics.

Additional resources are provided at http://study.sagepub.com/drozdova.

Technical Note: The log of zero is undefined and we will have to account for this in calculations involving zero probability states. Fortunately, in our context it is mathematically sound to define zero times the log of zero to be zero ($0 \times \log(0) = 0$). Thus, the entropy formula introduced earlier in this chapter remains well-defined even for systems where some of the states have zero probability ($p_i = 0$). We will encounter this scenario when some combinations of independent and dependent variable values are not observed in a case study. Because the log of zero is undefined, however, evaluating $0 \times \log(0)$ is not something that most computers handle automatically. We manage this problem by approximating zero with a very small number (0.00001) in these situations. (See Chapter 4 for additional discussion and other implementation details.)

3

Case Selection

Before we can turn to our much-anticipated step-by-step guide to using information analysis for comparative case studies, we need to pause for a serious conversation about case selection. It should go without saying that the selection of cases is a critical element of case study research strategies. But this subject is of such paramount importance that we need to devote a full chapter to its meanings and methods. Of course, case selection is an important issue for large-N studies as well. In that world, however, there is a simple clarion call for making sure that case selection is plausibly random or, failing that, for the use of compensatory quantitative techniques. Small-n work, by definition, is much more vulnerable to case selection issues. It is essential that we spell out some of these challenges and their relationship to the information metrics before we move on to the actual mechanics of applying information theory to comparative case studies.

All research designs have limitations. The authors of case studies need to be aware of the limitations of their research design and any potential biases in their case selection to account for them when interpreting the findings and drawing more general inferences. Likewise, the information approach, as with any analysis, is not immune to the challenges of missing data and coding issues.

This chapter discusses research design issues and case selection strategies for maximizing leverage from the use of information metrics in comparative case studies. It addresses key challenges regarding theoretically driven qualitative case selection relative to the random sampling techniques more commonly associated with quantitative methods. While it remains important to be explicitly aware of case selection issues, a key advantage of our information-theoretic method is that it is agnostic to the underlying case selection strategy. It offers an effective, systematic, and quantified analysis of results from whatever the given cases are.

We address the issues of case selection and coding here, as well as in the context of our more hands-on demonstration of information theory techniques in Chapter 4, and the discussion of sensitivity analysis in Chapter 6. While we will survey some of the more important and overarching case selection issues, this necessarily brief discussion cannot serve as a full treatment of the manifold issues of research design and case selection. Instead, our primary focus is on those critical places where research design and information theory intersect.

Research Design and Information Theory

As we discussed in Chapter 1, the quest to address the challenges of consequential decision making under high uncertainty has revolutionized analytics in many fields, from physics and computer science to case study research in the social sciences. Information theory provided a quantitative universal measure of uncertainty, which was labeled "information entropy," and a measure of how much knowledge of one variable reduced uncertainty about another, which was labeled "mutual information." The fundamental nature of these measures made them applicable across many fields. Now, as we extend their application to comparative case studies, it is essential to better understand how these studies are designed and conducted—to appropriately quantify the information inputs and evaluate the findings and implications. Because our focus is on small-*n* analytics, the selection of cases is especially important. It will always be challenging to generalize from such samples, which remain largely in the domain of what Alexander George termed "contingent generalization":

> For purposes of diagnosis and contingent prediction in a short-term, current problem, decision-makers need—and *a fortiori* policy scientists need—theoretical conclusions of a more sophisticated order: conclusions that identify how relevant situational variables change and vary according to circumstances. We call conclusions of this kind "contingent generalizations." (George & Smoke, 1974, p. 636)

The primary purpose of this chapter, then, is to complement Chapter 2's conceptual explanation of the information-theoretic measures with a discussion of the relevant key elements and principles of case studies themselves. In the context of research design, we focus especially on the selection and coding of cases, which shape the inputs for the information analytics as well as a study's overall inferential potential. This will create a foundation with all of the conceptual building blocks in place for learning our information method for comparative case studies. We then introduce the method step by step in Chapter 4, with more examples and advanced materials in further chapters.

The information-theoretic metrics travel naturally across disciplines because they address fundamental scientific and practical problems. The need to quantify and gauge uncertainty is shared by case studies as much as the physical and informatics fields where information theory originated. A research design addresses such challenges by applying basic principles of the scientific method. The process starts with a clear purpose and a research question aligned to that purpose. Empirical research, whether quantitative or qualitative, is essentially about using evidence to evaluate logical arguments. The arguments derive from theories in the form of hypotheses or prospective answers to the research question. Hypotheses may be descriptive, predictive, or explanatory. Specific hypotheses about relationships between dependent and independent variables are evaluated employing scientific methods. These methods typically involve systematic operationalization of concepts, measurement, data collection, and analysis procedures. Their use allows the researcher to establish the reliability, validity, and uncertainty (or confidence levels) of the findings. Rich details may emerge, especially from in-depth field or archival case studies, but in principle, the findings of a study come down to whether the evidence supports a hypothesis or not and what may be inferred as a result.

In principle, theories are evaluated by experimentation or observation (Van Evera, 1997, pp. 27–43). Springing from physical sciences, experimentation has been adapted into social science domains as well. Typical observational tests come in two varieties: large-N or case studies. Large-N designs enable the identification of statistically significant patterns and generalizations. Alternatively, small(er)-n case studies offer the advantage of in-depth investigation into causality and other aspects of real events but typically with limited inference and contingent generalization (George & Bennett, 2005). This generates three basic empirical testing methods: experimentation, observation using large-N statistical analysis, and observation using small-n case study analysis.

Experimental designs enable increased controls and statistical confidence levels in the testing of causal relationships in laboratory-type settings, but they often trade off greater controls for lesser external validity as lab conditions tend to strip away many complexities of the real world. Designs known as natural experiments allow researchers to analyze unfolding empirical situations consistent with aspects of an experiment (when certain variables can be said to be controlled by some design approximation). Such studies tend to gain external validity but at the expense of reduced controls and increased uncertainty. Hybrid designs that combine elements of experimentation and observation may interfere with what is being observed or policy decisions being made. They must guard against undue influence. Finally, observational designs do not try to control the environment they are observing but face the challenges of scope and inference from the collected data. Case studies probe deep causal patterns, challenge assumptions, and generate new hypotheses. They check verisimilitude between theory and reality by closely evaluating explanations relative to known facts in context (Bueno de Mesquita, 2002).

Information analysis emphasizes scientific research principles: design first, analyze second, and conclude based on logic and evidence. Large-N analysis may tempt the researcher to inappropriately experiment with different formulations and functional forms in the pursuit of statistical significance. Methodologies for systematic qualitative research, such as structured-focused comparison, start with research design, the outcome of interest, and the identification of theoretically relevant factors (see, e.g., Brady & Collier, 2010; George & Bennett, 2005; King, Keohane, & Verba, 1994; Yin, 2014). Such methods predefine operationalizations and guide the selection of the appropriate cases. Only then should the analyst turn to coding. With the cases analyzed and the coding completed, the analyst can then apply the information metrics to help provide a systematic understanding of the comparative case study results.

Robert K. Yin (2004), a leading scholar and developer of case study research methodologies, argues that "the case study method does not fall cleanly within the province of either quantitative or qualitative methods. In fact, how the case study method is to be categorized among other social science methods has been the subject of extensive writing." He argues that, although "no method of social science research, by definition, can replicate the scientific method in the natural sciences," emulating the principles of scientific research produces strong case study research. This emulation means "starting with explicit research questions, using a research design to address these questions, collecting and fairly presenting evidence to support interpretations, and referencing related research to aid in defining questions and drawing conclusions" (p. xix).

Logic and Evidence: Diverse Approaches, Common Standards

An influential debate about the logic of inquiry and the limits of inference in qualitative research (Brady & Collier, 2010; King et al., 1994) has pushed scholars to better appreciate scientific standards as well as the nuanced insights of case studies. This debate has emphasized the need to make case studies systematic and create tools, standards, and approaches that will enable analytic generalizations and the broader accumulation of knowledge (Yin, 2014).

The logic of scientific inquiry connects the research questions and objectives to the specifics of study design chosen to address them. Diverse approaches for gaining systematic insights and drawing appropriate inferences from case studies share the core standards of scientific research. Case selection is central to these comparative designs. Yin (2014) points out that case selection is not an exercise in sampling such as for survey research or other large-N endeavors. He argues that the logic of analytic inference and theory development should guide case selection, not the logic of statistical sampling from a population. Scholarly perspectives on this may differ, but the importance of setting up cases in order to draw valid inferences or conclusions from a study remains.

Scientific scholarship stands on logic and evidence—not on personal tastes, policy preferences, unchecked assumptions, hopes, or other unscientific inclinations. A solid research design and professional ethics serve to limit subjectivity. Replication and more in-depth exploration build further confidence in our knowledge.

Confidence in our findings is strengthened by the complementarities of different methods. Case study methods offer insights through detailed analyses of events in context, often leveraging archival research and varieties of data to generate or probe deep explanations of complex phenomena. At the end of the day, every research method has some blind spots, and the use of complementary methods and tools enables us to better leverage the strengths and compensate for the potential shortcomings of each. Whereas case study approaches can illuminate the internal workings of specific sets of events to identify theory-relevant patterns, statistical analysis probes broader generalities in how variables relate to one another across similar circumstances. Other approaches can examine the logic of action linking the observations and the explanations of reality to further bolster our understanding (Bueno de Mesquita, 2002).

Consistent with these purposes, information analytics add further tools to the scholarly toolbox. But case selection remains a critical element in qualitative research strategies for improving inference and leverage from comparative case studies. Each of these analytic concepts, inference and leverage, merits a more focused discussion.

Inference

Inference refers to the ability to extract more general implications from a subset of cases. Our basic philosophical approach in this book is consistent with the position that it is indeed possible to make valid inferences from qualitative case study research. These inferences may be of descriptive or causal nature, enabled by appropriate research design and, as with any research, tempered by careful evaluation of contingencies, limitations, and uncertainty. Small sample inference from case studies is primarily a domain of what George calls "contingent generalizations" (George & Smoke, 1974; George & Bennett, 2005) and Yin (2011, 2014) calls "analytic generalization." With these cautions, inferences can be drawn.

The structured-focused comparison methodology provides a helpful generic conceptualization of a case in scientific studies designed for drawing inferences from a small set of cases: *A case is defined as an instance of a class of events* (George & Bennett, 2005, p. 17). A "class of events" is a phenomenon of interest that can be identified in many different instances with variation in both the outcomes and the theoretically interesting independent factors. The variability across cases leads to uncertainty about the relationships between the variables involved, such as what factors cause or may be indicative of different outcomes in wars, different learning outcomes in education programs, poverty alleviation efforts, and so on. Contingent generalizations from the carefully selected cases may then extend to the relevant class of events depending on the study's theoretical construction and empirical scope.

Researchers select specific cases to develop theory (or "generic knowledge") regarding the causes or implications of similarities, differences, or other theoretically relevant characteristics among instances (cases) of that class of events (George & Bennett, 2005, p. 18).

Consistent with this more general perspective on cases and case selection, Yin (2014) emphasizes that cases selected for case study research are not equivalent to sampling units for statistical analysis. Although a set of cases could be a random sample, and we address how this can be done in a theory-driven comparative case study setting later in this chapter, in most studies, the selection of cases will not be random. These concepts and selection techniques are distinct not only because small *ns* are typically insufficient to serve as an adequately sized sample to be statistically representative of any larger population—but ultimately because case selection is a different mode of inquiry. Thinking conceptually about generalization in terms of implications beyond the immediate data, Yin explicitly distinguishes between analytic and statistical generalizations, emphasizing the inherent value and validity of small-*n analytic* generalization appropriate for the case study world.

Analytic generalization is a two-step process: "The first involves a conceptual claim whereby investigators show how their study's findings are likely to inform a particular set of concepts, theoretical constructs, or hypothesized sequence of events. The second involves applying the same theory to implicate other similar situations where similar concepts might be relevant" (Yin, 2011, p. 100; see also Yin, 2014, chap. 2). The key idea is that cases should not be thought of in statistical terms as samples from which to generalize to populations—rather, case studies seek to develop and discuss how findings might have implications for an improved understanding of particular concepts and patterns derived from deep knowledge of cases framed in context and conditions of study design. Cases are carefully chosen for opportunities to "shed empirical light about some theoretical concepts or principles, not unlike the motive of a laboratory investigator in conceiving of and then conducting a new experiment. In this sense, both a case study and an experiment may have an interest in going beyond the specific case or experiment. Both kinds of studies are likely to strive for generalizable findings or lessons learned—that is, analytic generalizations—that go beyond the setting for the specific experiment that has been studied" (Yin, 2014, p. 40).

Such lessons learned could be in the form of new/broadly applicable explanations or working hypotheses to reinterpret the findings of other studies, diagnose new situations, or to identify new research directions. Analytic generalizations, Yin (2014) argues, operate "at a conceptual level higher than that of the specific case" and thus may serve to advance theoretical concepts as well as inform other relevant practical situations (Yin, 2014, p. 41). For example, scholars and practitioners may want to learn from history. They may draw on the study of archival records of particular cases of phenomena of interest (wars, foreign aid programs, influential individuals or events, etc.). To go beyond past instances, however, approaches amenable to analytic generalization will be required for deriving valid lessons with the potential to inform future decisions.

Our information metrics serve the goals of better identifying what is learned from the given case studies with measures of uncertainty that can inform such analytic or contingent generalizations. These metrics add a new and effective way for systematizing findings, disciplining analytic generalizations, and handling uncertainty in qualitative comparative case studies.

Scholars may debate the finer points but generally agree on the goals of producing and improving valid inferences from case studies. King et al. (1994, pp. 7–9) explain the logic of inference shared across many different methods and disciplines in terms of four principles: One, the goal is inference about the world on the basis of empirical information. Two, the procedures are public, so scholars can check and build on one another's work. Three, the content is the method—the systematic procedures that make it possible to draw reliable and valid conclusions and inferences from the collected and analyzed data. Four, the conclusions are uncertain. And it is that uncertainty that is so difficult to ascertain by qualitative methods alone, the problem we address with information metrics.

Leverage

Beyond the content of knowledge and its inferential value, scholars often seek to learn as much as possible from a study—to maximize leverage. Leverage here means how much is learned or explained by a given set of cases and variables analyzed. Leverage over a research problem is considered high when complex effects can be explained with a single or relatively few causal variables. Leverage also reflects the potential of variables or tools to eliminate rival explanations. Because the leverage of any particular variable in explaining multifaceted real-world problems tends to be relatively low, attaining high leverage has been called "one of the most important achievements of all social science"—"good social science seeks to increase the significance of what is explained relative to the information used in the explanation" (King et al., 1994, pp. 29–30).

Our information analytics support this goal by offering tools to understand and improve the leverage of a given set of comparative cases. Maximizing leverage basically means explaining as much as possible with as little as possible.

Information-theoretic metrics offer quantifiable, systematic, and comparable measures of leverage, among other indicators. By telling us how informative each variable is about the outcome, they help us identify the variables with highest leverage. The independent variables can be comparatively evaluated and clearly ranked in terms of their relative impact.

Brady, Collier, and Seawright (2010, pp. 177–182) explore the tools for descriptive inference and the sources of leverage for eliminating rival explanations in causal inference. They point to several distinct advantages of qualitative case studies. In particular, qualitative measures (such as nominal descriptions and patterns derived from process tracing and other qualitative analytics) are more direct. Qualitative measures require fewer assumptions about underlying logical relationships compared to numerical measures for traditional statistical techniques where more quantitative precision may be achieved at the expense of unrealistic or unverified assumptions. Small-*n* case studies are better suited for analytic leverage and analytic inference enabled by detailed analysis of qualitative data. This aligns with information analytics that can convey the impact of rich contextual findings with relatively simple and straightforward numerical indicators of their information content and leverage.

Research leverage can be increased in several ways. The theory can be improved so that it generates more observable and measurable implications from its hypotheses. Better data could make more of such implications observable and usable to evaluate the theory. New approaches could enable learning more from the existing data. (King et al., 1994, p. 30) The core challenge revolves around obtaining more knowledge from the available information and evaluating the uncertainty of the results. This is the need our information and uncertainty metrics fill.

Analysts will draw inferences from small-*n* case studies, and practitioners will use them. Our argument is that they should do so guided by more concrete metrics, rather than relying only on subjective assessment. The systematic and replicable information-theoretic measures we provide can help make the results of small-*n* studies much clearer. Ultimately, however, while information metrics can improve what is learned from the given case studies they cannot remove the underlying challenges of drawing inferences from a small set of cases. How those cases are selected is critical to the inferential potential of the study.

Case Selection Strategies and Challenges

Purposes, Criteria, Debates

Case study methodologies enable a deep understanding of the nuances, patterns, and meanings of social behavior achieved through investigations of particular individuals or situations under specified contextual conditions.

There has been much debate about generalization from case studies. Inference from small numbers of cases is always difficult and subject to critical questions about case selection and conditions under which the insights drawn may apply beyond the immediate data to inform our understanding of the broader phenomena. These challenges as well as the advantages of deeper insights from case studies make it incumbent upon scholars to explain the logic of their inquiry, justify their choice of cases in that context, and characterize the relevant dimensions so that the readers may appropriately frame any broader implications drawn from the study.

Additionally, scholars from many disciplines involved in qualitative research have emphasized the need for cumulative case study work, including the systematic, documented, and replicable choices of cases and study designs to facilitate the growth of knowledge over time and across many studies (see, e.g., Brady & Collier, 2010; Dunbar & Starbuck, 2006; George & Bennett, 2005; Gomm, Hammersley, & Foster, 2000; King et al., 1994; Yin, 2011).

And so, for a variety of case study purposes—for example, from understanding the details of a case at hand to building or testing theories, exploring conditions and contingent relationships, and accumulating knowledge from comparisons of multiple cases—case selection remains critical to the ability to derive greater value from a study. This is especially true if the study is meant to have implications beyond the immediate data collected.

Two interrelated perspectives inform the strategies and criteria for case selection:

- *Information (content)* considerations shape selection strategies with a focus on how well the cases serve for acquiring and communicating knowledge relative to a study's intended practical or theoretical purposes.
- *Replication (process)* considerations shape selection strategies with a focus on enabling systematic procedures for meaningful multiple-case designs and inferences from comparative analysis.

These complementary considerations frame the applicability and usefulness of information metrics for systematizing and evaluating findings. They also set criteria for assessing the appropriateness of selected variables for their information content, regardless of the case selection strategy chosen.

There are many different legitimate and appropriate criteria for selecting cases. Van Evera (1997, p. 88) synthesizes a broad range of case study research to show how different purposes align with informational criteria for case selection. For example, a study focused on developing or testing cutting-edge theoretical notions may have significantly different case selection requirements than a study focused on learning applicable lessons and communicating best practices for immediate policy implementation. The specific purposes might include testing theories, inferring theories, inferring antecedent conditions, testing conditions, and studying cases of intrinsic importance such as for policy-relevant knowledge. There is a very wide range of case selection criteria that might map onto these purposes: selecting cases with a focus on data richness, identifying cases with extreme values on critical independent or dependent variables, choosing cases with large within-case variation on the variables of interest, focusing on cases for which competing theories make divergent predictions about the case outcomes, selecting cases with a clear resemblance to current policy problems, choosing cases that are thought to have prototypical case characteristics, matching cases to create cross-case controlled comparison, investigating cases with outcomes that are unexplained by other theories, focusing on cases of intrinsic importance, selecting cases that are particularly appropriate for replicating previous tests, or looking for cases that are configured to allow a new type of test. The important thing is that the analysts be aware of their particular research needs and that case selection criteria are developed intentionally and appropriately. A clear awareness of the case selection criteria is essential for making appropriate inferences from the cases.

From the replication standpoint, Yin (2014) discusses a conceptually different but complementary set of guidelines for case selection, namely to satisfy what he calls "replication, not sampling, logic for multiple-case studies" (p. 57). Every case should be selected to serve a specific purpose within the overall study design and scope of inquiry. He argues that, in addition to theoretical or other informational purposes, the cases should be treated not unlike multiple experiments, enabling replication. As in structured-focused comparison, the same procedures should apply and be replicable for each of the cases to enable systematic data collection and analysis procedures with meaningful cross-case comparisons and analytic inference as a result.

If the procedures are designed for replication and well documented, even doing one case at a time can serve the goals of further replication and knowledge accumulation. Replication may be *literal,* whereby cases are selected to test hypotheses about the same results produced by similar conditions, or *theoretical,* whereby cases are selected to examine contrary results but for predictable reasons. Sets of cases are then built to examine sets of propositions and conditions under which particular types of outcomes are expected as specified by the study's design. The theoretical framework can then become a vehicle for generalizing to new cases or developing new theoretical perspectives (Yin, 2014).

Now, as we move from these design considerations to the practicalities of data collection and coding, it is useful to contrast three broad approaches to case selection: theoretical (theory-driven) case selection, random (within specified conditions) case selection, and intentionally biased case selection.

Theoretical Case Selection Strategies

Theory-driven case selection strategies use the observable implications of theory to guide data collection. Theory serves to focus the inquiry and help distinguish the relevant from the irrelevant facts—a critical consideration in case studies where a multitude of information could potentially serve as data. Theory and empirical research are tightly connected in case study work. Theory guides the types of evidence that are relevant and appropriate for testing the study's hypotheses. Data considerations discipline theoretical conclusions that must be consistent with and confined to the scope of evidence considered.

The particulars of a theory being developed or tested by a case study also clarify the distinction between a "case" (i.e., a real-life set of events from which data will be drawn), and the "case study," which will be a more narrowly scoped research inquiry focused on specific propositions and purposes of the investigation and consisting of the research question, theoretical perspectives, empirical findings, interpretations, and conclusions consistent with the predetermined design (Yin, 2004).

For example, *The Strategy of Campaigning* (Skinner, Kudelia, Bueno de Mesquita, & Rice, 2008) analyzes the parallel cases of two politicians, each of whom demonstrated a remarkable political resurrection after a number of failures by winning the highest leadership office in his respective superpower nation through a democratic process. These unlikely protagonists are Ronald Reagan and Boris Yeltsin, and the book explains their respective careers and changes in the world that they advanced. The *n* of two is very small but strategically selected. The study leverages the rich histories and archival documents for theoretical advancement. It moves beyond accounts of political campaigning to set out questions and a framework for specifying generalizations about the strategies of campaigning investigated through these unique cases. The approach considers a cross-national theory of campaigning and focuses on the general question of "how politicians whose ideas are seemingly at odds with mainstream political thought nevertheless rise to hold the highest office in the land" (Skinner et al., 2008, p. 5). As this phenomenon can happen anywhere and provides insights into politics at large, the study's implications reach beyond its two specific cases, enabled by a carefully crafted theoretical argument and an empirical strategy to investigate the theoretical conditions that shape the answer to the research question (and the fates of nations).

Random Selection Strategies

Randomness is a powerful approach for selecting observations, typically for large-N studies, because it provides a selection procedure such that the odds of a selection rule correlating with any observed variable are negligibly small (King et al., 1994, pp. 124–128). The principle of a random selection procedure is that any element in the population being studied has an equal chance of being drawn into the sample. The procedure is valued for its ability to remove subjective biases. It may be uncomfortable to say the least for scholars trained in mathematical analysis of stochastic processes and other probabilistic events to let go of random selection.

Many case study designs, however, as already discussed, explicitly abandon randomness for an intentional theory-driven selection to enhance analytic generalization. To help bridge this transition, we would like to reemphasize that different designs and selection strategies are appropriate for different studies, and each can be accomplished systematically following the scientific principles we outlined earlier.

In the context of comparative case studies, there is a way to leverage the advantages of random selection combined with the deliberate specification of the theory-relevant conditions to be explored. The approach is to conceptually define the general conditions guiding case selection (through a deliberate procedure defined by the research design) and then randomly select a number of specific cases that fit those conditions. This procedure is consistent with random selection because in this context, it means that every potential unit (case) that satisfies the conditions (criteria) has an equal probability of selection into the study's set of cases, and successive choices are independent (King et al., 1994, p. 124).

For example, Drozdova (2008) used a similar approach to first establish theoretical dimensions for case selection and then selected cases for in-depth comparative case study based on those dimensions. The study used a complementary application of information theory to explore research questions about how organizations use technology and human networks to survive in different environments. An information analysis of a variety of theoretically driven factors determined the two dominant theoretical dimensions for studying organizational survival strategies. These dimensions were hostility characteristics of the environment (particularly adversarial relationships among organizations in their institutional rather than natural environment) and organizational missions (particularly shaped primarily by ideological rather than monetary or other such motivations). The environmental hostility and organizational mission dimensions were then used as a framework for selecting a small n of contrasting cases for in-depth comparative investigation. Organizations that fit the theoretically determined criteria were selected randomly in the sense that any one that fit had in principle an equal chance of being selected. This approach generated broader implications for business and counterterrorism organizations, among others, and contributed the information-theoretic framework for cases selection.

Biased or Intentional Selection Strategies

Biased selection may sound alarm bells. Bias is generally considered a source of systematic error in research or, more commonly, some subjective interference that may cloud our ability to see things clearly in empirical terms. The intentional selection of cases that, for example, are known to confirm one's theory may create a skewed understanding of the world.

In fact, however, appropriately and intentionally biased case selection can provide significant research leverage. When cases are carefully chosen following some of the strategies outlined earlier, inferences can be more confidently drawn. For example, with a "least-likely" case selection strategy, cases are chosen with characteristics that give us a theoretical expectation that it is unlikely that the explanatory factor of interest will have a significant impact (Eckstein, 1975). If, even in this biased sample, the factor shows a strong effect, we can think it much more likely that the factor will be important in the more general population.

Alternatively, we may be at a point in some scientific research agenda where we simply need to demonstrate that some complex or unusual causal hypothesis is plausible and thus worthy of more difficult or costly experiments or studies. In that scenario, we might choose a set of cases where theoretical expectations lead us to strongly expect to find the posited relationship. If the effect fails to show even in this highly favorable and protected test, we can more confidently avoid the more costly studies (Eckstein, 1975). The inferential leverage is greater from this biased test than it would have been from a random small-n test in which low-frequency events are unlikely to show themselves.

The critical thing, of course, is that researchers be intentional and transparent about the purposes and nature of their case selection strategy. One way or another, scholars must look out for biases and account for them to maintain the scientific standards and integrity of their research.

Here we may point to contrasting examples highlighting the downsides of biased case selection or the advantages of such designs under different circumstances. On the downside, picking cases because they are consistent with a theory may lead investigators to miss the cases that could refute the theory, leading to invalid, incomplete, or misleading conclusions. On the upside, a deeper investigation of the conditions shaping theory's predictions can help explore certain especially important aspects of the theory at hand. This can be very beneficial as long as the researcher is upfront about the selection method and its implications.

Authors of case studies should be well aware of the biases in their case selection and explicitly address them by explaining the rationale and ensuring valid interpretations and conclusions. Information analysis advances these goals. It is a tool to make the assessment of comparative cases more systematic and transparent. As we show in Chapter 6, it also offers a method to more clearly understand the impact of specific cases on the analytic results.

Coding Cases

Once cases are selected, the proper way to conduct a structured-focused comparative case study is to develop a theoretically derived and consistent set of questions to ask of each case. The specific content of these questions will be particular to the issue being explored and the theoretical foundations of the subject area. The overarching technical requirement for this approach is that the answers to the question are amenable to the assignment of numerical and ultimately binary values.

Outcomes, of course, can have multiple possible states. As we will show, they can still be systematically coded as binary. Information metrics can be used for the analysis of more complex permutations and combinatorics, but we start with a straightforward and powerful binary approach in this book. There is also a strong tradition of binary quantification in the qualitative case analysis (QCA) literature, which we address in Chapter 7.

To produce the data for the information analysis, one must be able to precisely define, in a measurable way, what exactly constitutes a positive occurrence of a factor and what exactly constitutes a successful outcome. The researcher determines these "True" categories in the context of the case studies guided by the comparative research design. This will be used in creating truth tables and quantified data as part of the information method further explained in Chapter 4.

The binary categorization is a simple application of logical operators: "True" or "Not True," where all possibilities other than True are designated as "False." This approach divides all the possible states of a variable into two mutually exclusive categories. True indicates the presence of a factor or the success of an outcome. When there is enough evidence to meet the "True" definition, the variable is coded as 1 or otherwise as 0. The two defined categories of possible outcomes must be mutually exclusive, and the researcher must be able to systematically—unambiguously, validly, and reliably—assign what counts as a "1" in order for the counts to be accurate and useful.

Many variables are naturally conducive to 0/1 coding. A condition is either present or it isn't. There are many variables for which this dichotomization will be reasonably straightforward: male/female, drug/placebo, resident/nonresident.

Other real-world phenomena involve a range of possibilities with many shades of meaning. The operational approach in those cases is to precisely and measurably define what constitutes "True." Where variables are more naturally continuous, the key to binary quantification is identifying the critical cut point that divides the 0/1 coding: If the subject's age is greater than 18, the "adult" variable is coded as "True"; if there are more than 6 hours of sunlight, the "sunny" variable is coded as "True"; the "high blood pressure" variable is coded as "True" if systolic blood pressure is greater than 140 mmHg. For the purposes of building a truth table, when the specified conditions are met, the variable is coded as True. All other states are then coded as False.

Challenges may arise in defining each positive category in a way that is meaningful and informative as well as practical, given the often complex and sometimes ambiguous nature of qualitative case study evidence. Theory, research objectives, and subject matter knowledge will be critical for helping resolve these questions.

The selection of a combination of empirically well-documented cases and variables amenable to clear binary classification covering all possible combinations of factors and outcome values facilitates the knowledge gain from qualitative data.

Quantifying the cases into binary codes creates a comprehensive yet compact and indicative overview of the results that then become inputs for our information analytics. The problems of drawing inference from a small sample are preserved in quantification, but information analytics add substantial value in understanding and disciplining the results. Information analysis of comparative case studies cannot avoid the underlying studies' errors of conceptualization or case selection. The researcher remains responsible to ensure that the theoretically appropriate independent and dependent variables have been identified and that the cases are appropriately reflective of the larger phenomena. But information analysis can improve the likelihood that such errors are caught as well as enhance leverage and learning from small-n analytics.

Case Selection and the Advantages of Information-Theoretic Analysis

Our initial impetus for developing this approach arose from a concern about the widespread lack of systematic across-case evaluation of comparative case study findings. Quantitative metrics can help discipline subjective case study analysis, but it is also important that they do not provide a false sense of precision or otherwise mislead.

Case studies are used by policy makers and scholars across many disciplines. The research and philosophical grounding for case study analysis, as well as the appropriate ways to conduct and present case study research, have been covered from a number of different angles. Nonetheless, weakly structured and unsystematically presented case studies seem to be the norm rather than the exception. We began our current project on information theory with a reanalysis of three prominent examples of structured-focused case studies in political science (Drozdova & Gaubatz, 2014). All three of these studies were carefully structured and conducted by distinguished scholars. In each of these examples, however, there was a notable lack of systematic assessment in the presentation of cases. In two of the examples, tables of results were presented without any analytic overview. In the third case, no summary table was even provided. The lack of a clear comparative case summary is, alas, a common feature of subjective small-*n* studies.

Effective Leverage From Any, Even Biased, Case Selection

The information-theoretic approach works regardless of the case selection strategy. Information analytics can help clarify the impact of different variables and case selection strategies. From the information perspective of case selection criteria we discussed, our approach illuminates the relative information content of the different variables through quantifiable measures of uncertainty and mutual information contained in the relationships between independent and dependent variables. From the replicability perspective, quantification forces a more orderly presentation and evaluation of results, enabling more systematic comparisons while preserving and building on the underlying richness and nuance of comparative case studies.

For the most informative results and the highest leverage, it is generally advisable to select cases with the greatest possible variation in the values of both the dependent and independent variables. It is also typically best to avoid sets of cases that all share the same outcome (i.e., all successes or all failures). This type of case selection bias is known as selection on the dependent variable. Because information metrics are designed to help us understand how variation in the independent variables relates to variation in the dependent variable (case outcomes), sets of cases with only uniform outcomes will not be useful for distinguishing the factors that will best improve our ability to correctly anticipate the outcome of an uncertain process.

Selecting on the dependent variable is a particularly common failing in policy analysis, as we discussed at the end of Chapter 2. By construction, our information metrics highlight the dangers of selecting cases based on a single outcome type, since a lack of variation in either the independent or dependent variable will eliminate the potential for uncertainty reduction. Limited variation in an independent variable will reduce its information content and thus its ability to tell us about variation in the dependent variable. If there is no variation in the outcome, there will be no uncertainty and thus no possibility for uncertainty reduction.

Complementarities of Information Metrics With Structured-Focused Comparison

Among the qualitative case study methodologies designed to make case research systematic and inferential, the rigorous structured-focused comparison is especially well suited for enhancement with information-theoretic techniques. By modeling and exploring complex contingent generalizations within the framework of typological theories, the structured-focused approach demands discipline and replicability in the procedures that make the variables readily quantifiable for information metrics, while retaining the deep knowledge and underlying subtlety that case studies provide.

The procedures George and Bennett (2005) recommend for developing typological theories foster cross-case comparisons as well as systematic and replicable within-case analyses. Typological approaches guide researchers through matching the alternative research designs with historical cases toward maximizing leverage from their theoretically chosen sets of cases. Structured-focused comparisons driven by typological theories can also "guide researchers toward questions and research designs whose results will be pertinent to problems faced by policymakers . . . to provide policymakers with 'generic knowledge' that will help them form effective strategies" (p. 9). These scientific as well as practical purposes require tools for managing uncertainty and learning systematically from the cases we have. In the context of structured-focused comparisons information metrics fill this need. In Chapter 4, we use a prominent example of a structured-focused comparison to demonstrate in detail how to apply the information-theoretic measures to comparative case studies.

Conclusion

Research design and case selection are a critical part of all comparative case studies. Information analytics cannot eliminate all of the underlying challenges of small-*n* studies, so understanding matters of design and case selection remains essential. Information metrics do enable clearer insights and more systematic learning from comparative case studies. Moreover, these methods can be effective regardless of underlying case selection styles and designs as long as the researcher is careful and intentional about these choices. We will return to these issues in Chapter 6, where we look at several approaches to understanding the sensitivity of information metrics to case selection strategies.

The bottom line is that it is essential that case study selection be performed with intentionality, transparency, and awareness. How you pick your cases will have an effect both on the outcomes and on the kinds of inferences you can draw from cases to the real world. Obviously, small-n research cannot fall back on the law of large numbers. It is likely in small-n analysis that case acquisition is relatively expensive, so finding cases by trial and error, or even just replacing cases that are found inappropriate, is often not an option.

Research design is a much covered topic. There are many excellent books on research design and case study (see, e.g., Creswell, 2013; Gorard, 2013; Hulley, Cummings, Browner, Grady, & Newman, 2013; Yin, 2014). These should be consulted, of course, at the beginning of the process, rather than mined for support ex post.

In the next chapter, we embark on a step-by-step implementation of information analytics for assessing case study results. To facilitate this effort, we will draw on a prominent example of comparative case study from Alexander L. George, who, as we saw in Chapter 1, was a primary architect of the method of structured-focused comparison.

Additional resources are provided at http://study.sagepub.com/drozdova.

The Information Method— If You Can Count, You Can Do It

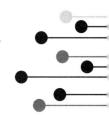

I n this chapter, we present a simple step-by-step guide to information analysis for comparative case studies. *The fundamental steps are quantify, count, compute, and compare.* These four procedures apply the information and case study concepts we have outlined in the first three chapters.

We demonstrate the information method at work and its analytic leverage with a reexamination of a prominent example of comparative case study, *The Limits of Coercive Diplomacy,* by Alexander George and William Simons (1994). As we work through the step-by-step procedure for this example, we show how information analytics can provide a systematic quantitative understanding of the strengths and limitations of structured-focused comparisons and can reduce the uncertainty often associated with their results.

Information analytics enhance case findings by *quantitatively* answering the following questions: What is the magnitude of uncertainty? How much can we learn about an uncertain outcome given an observed factor that is theorized to be related to the outcome? What are the relative impacts of multiple factors on the outcome? What factors are most useful to know to reduce the outcome uncertainty? What is the impact of the individual cases on the analytic conclusions? The answers to these questions can offer actionable knowledge for both research and practice.

The information method begins with the identification of a set of appropriate cases, an outcome of interest (the dependent variable), and the specific factors (independent variables) to be analyzed in each case. The method uses binary values to quantify the variables and simple counts to calculate the uncertainty measures of information entropy and mutual information. These measures inform a systematic understanding of the outcomes and provide a clear metric for the knowledge gained from comparing cases. The binary quantification reflects the original approach of measuring information in bits, as explained in Chapter 1.

As in Chapter 2, we are going to present the method in two different ways. First, we work out the information metrics building up from the total, joint, and conditional probabilities. Then, we demonstrate a shortcut approach using the joint probabilities from the *abcd* table (as in Table 2.3) to calculate the information metrics from the frequency counts in just one step.

Quantify: Setting Up a Truth Table for Comparative Case Analysis

Principles and Data

By systematically assessing uncertainty, information measures help us go beyond subjective eyeballing of qualitative results toward a better understanding of the contribution of each factor to reducing uncertainty about the outcome studied.

By research design, the dependent variable that the cases seek to explain is called an "outcome." It is defined in terms of a successful outcome or not. All other factors that are theorized to be related to the outcome are defined in terms of whether the condition or attribute represented by each independent variable is present or not. As discussed in Chapter 3, the determination of what it means to be "successful" or "present" is made systematically based on theoretical understanding, specific definitions, and the evidence collected in the cases.

The method we propose uses simple frequency counts to calculate the basic probability concepts introduced in Chapter 2. In essence, the empirical probability of an outcome is the number of positive occurrences of an outcome divided by the total number of observations.

All variables are quantified using a binary approach, as discussed in Chapter 3. As always in research design, and especially for information analytics, each underlying variable must be defined precisely enough to enable meaningful, discrete, mutually exclusive binary categorization. This will be used for building truth tables to quantify the qualitative data.

A "truth table" is an analytical tool for evaluating logical arguments (see Truss, 1999, for an accessible but more in-depth discussion). Representationally, it is a matrix that records the values of True or False for the elements under investigation to systematically present the available information. These logical operators are quantified by assigning "1" to True or "0" (zero) to False. These 1s and 0s form the language of information theory as we learned in Chapter 2. The resulting truth table of 1s and 0s completely represents the observed states of each variable for each case in the given set of comparative case studies and thus becomes the basic data set for calculating the information metrics, analyzing patterns, and interpreting results.

For the purpose of comparative case study, the truth tables are built in two steps. First, it is necessary to assemble a data matrix with the cases on one dimension and the factors and outcomes on the other. This table will be populated, as demonstrated in Table 4.1, with the 1s and 0s to indicate for each case the presence or absence of each factor and the value of the outcome.

Table 4.1 Binary Data Table

VARIABLES Independent Variable X Dependent Variable Y		CASES				
		SCHOOL 1	SCHOOL 2	SCHOOL 3	SCHOOL 4	SCHOOL 5
X	Curriculum change	FALSE 0	TRUE 1	TRUE 1	TRUE 1	FALSE 0
Y	Improved test outcome	FALSE 0	TRUE 1	TRUE 1	FALSE 0	FALSE 0

Table 4.1 provides a basic example of a binary data table quantified using 1s and 0s. Let's suppose we are studying five schools that we believe are largely comparable and have been subject to some curriculum experiment. The independent variable (X) is whether the curriculum was changed at a given school. The dependent variable (Y) is whether some assessment test score has increased.

The second step is to assemble a truth table that looks at every combination of values for the independent and dependent variables. Table 4.2 takes the data from Table 4.1 and counts the number of occurrences of each permutation of independent and dependent variable values.

Albeit an intermediate step in information analytics, even creating a truth table is already a useful tool for comparative case study research. It forces one to systematize the underlying qualitative evidence, which may already reveal important insights or point to potential shortcomings of the research design. The requirement to unambiguously define and classify the qualitative evidence about the observed factors and outcomes forces order and discipline on the data. In this table, we can more clearly see what is present or absent in our data, note potential patterns of factor-outcome variation and what conditions are more or less frequently associated with what outcomes, examine missing values, and identify ambiguities that must be resolved for further analysis or accounted for in conclusions.

For example, in Table 4.2, we can see that our hypothetical study of schools lacks instances where no curriculum change ($X = 0$) is nevertheless associated with an improved test outcome ($Y = 1$). However, researchers should be aware of potential

Table 4.2 Summarized Truth Table Example

VARIABLES Independent Variable X Dependent Variable Y	Permutations			
	$X = 1$ $Y = 1$	$X = 0$ $Y = 1$	$X = 1$ $Y = 0$	$X = 0$ $Y = 0$
Number of cases	2	0	1	2

alternative explanations of such a pattern in the data. In principle, it is possible for test outcomes to improve in the absence of a curriculum change due to some other unobserved reasons (e.g., due to more knowledgeable students, cheating, or some other factors that are not captured by the data). One immediate advantage of a truth table is that it makes data patterns explicit, including identifying missing data and pointing to potential sources of uncertainty for further exploration.

A truth table is a more rigorous approach to evaluating qualitative comparative case studies than subjective interpretations too often used by case study authors to sum up their results. And it creates the quantitative data for more systematic analysis of what can be learned from the cases all together. We see this in practice in the example of George and Simons's (1994) classic set of cases on coercive diplomacy.

Example: Quantifying the Limits of Coercive Diplomacy

The Limits of Coercive Diplomacy edited by George and Simons (1994) explores the use of coercive strategies in international affairs whereby governments apply intimidation (short of war) to convince their opponents to comply with their policy wishes. The book has been cited as an exemplar of the structured-focused comparison methodology for qualitative case studies (George & Bennett, 2005). It analyzed seven cases of coercive diplomacy, three of which the authors of the case studies deemed successful, three others unsuccessful, and one ambiguous. The cases were used to assess the effect of nine different explanatory factors in an attempt to develop policy-relevant knowledge about the effectiveness of coercive threats in international diplomacy (Table 4.3 shows all the cases and factors).

A structured-focused comparison is a sufficient analytic tool when a set of cases clearly aligns to distinguish the impact of one or two central variables. Such clarity is rare, however, as even this prominent study demonstrates. The goal of making qualitative case studies more systematic can be further enhanced with the basic tools of information analysis. Just as in large-N regression methods, we need a rigorous and replicable way to assess the relative explanatory power of the different factors and their ability to clarify results, yet in a way that is accessible and useful for qualitative scholars. Information analytics enable greater clarity and metrics for assessing the impacts of multiple variables interacting in complex and uncertain ways, where a simple visual comparison of the results alone risks being insufficient or potentially misleading.

The Limits of Coercive Diplomacy illustrates these challenges and serves as an instructive example for explaining the information method step by step. Our first step is to set up and quantify a truth table containing data. Surprisingly, this important study stops short of providing clear conclusions about the comparative impact and importance of the factors around which it is structured and focused. It does provide a table summarizing the presence or absence of factors (independent variables) examined in the cases but, oddly, does not include the case outcomes (dependent variable values). Moreover, the actual analysis of the table is largely left to the reader's intuition. The problem is conveyed in Table 4.3, which displays George and Simons's (1994) data, with our addition of a "Success" row showing case outcomes. The advantage of this representation is that it serves as raw data for our truth table, the quantified version of which is shown in Table 4.4.

The process of creating these tables already forces discipline and clarity on the data. Possible patterns may be informative as well as useful for further study. For example, Table 4.3 contains many question marks among the factors and one ambiguous outcome, suggesting insufficiencies in the underlying data. All data points other than "+" and "Yes" are coded 0 in Table 4.4 to ensure a binary quantification, but that decision involves some uncertainty already, since a lack of evidence for a positive coding is not necessarily

Table 4.3 Summary Table for George and Simons' (1994) Qualitative Data on Coercive Diplomacy

FACTORS Independent Variables X	CASES						
	Pearl Harbor	Laos	Cuba	Vietnam	Libya	Nicaragua	Persian Gulf
Clarity of objective	+	+	+		?		+
Strong motivation	+	+	+	+	+	+	+
Asymmetry of motivation		+	+		?		
Sense of urgency	+	+	+				?
Strong leadership		+	+	+	+	+	+
Domestic support	+	?	+		+		+
International support	+	+	+				
Fear of unacceptable escalation		+	+		?	?	+
Clarity of terms	?	+	+				
Y: Success	No	Yes	Yes	No	Amb.	Yes	No

Data from George and Simons (1994, p. 288), with the addition of "Success" row showing case outcomes as described by the book's case studies, where "Amb." refers to "Ambiguous"; "+" indicates the presence of the row's factor in the corresponding column's case; "?" means that it is not clear whether the factor is present.

Table 4.4 Quantified Truth Table for George and Simons' (1994) Data on Coercive Diplomacy

	Clarity of Objective	Strong Motivation	Asymmetry of Motivation	Sense of Urgency	Strong Leadership	Domestic Support	International Support	Fear of Unacceptable Escalation	Clarity of Terms	Y: Success
Pearl Harbor	1	1	0	1	0	1	1	0	0	0
Laos	1	1	1	1	1	0	1	1	1	1
Cuba	1	1	1	1	1	1	1	1	1	1
Vietnam	0	1	0	0	1	0	0	0	0	0
Libya	0	1	0	0	1	1	0	0	0	0
Nicaragua	0	1	0	0	1	0	0	0	0	1
Persian Gulf	1	1	0	0	1	1	0	1	0	0
"1" frequency	0.57	1	0.29	0.43	0.86	0.57	0.43	0.43	0.29	0.43

Binary quantification of the data from George and Simons (1994) shown in Table 4.3. The presence of each factor indicated with a "+" (plus) in Table 4.3 is coded as 1 here; all others are coded as 0. Similarly, all outcomes "Yes" are coded as 1 and all others as 0.

equivalent to clear evidence to the contrary. As discussed in Chapter 3, the coding decisions must be theoretically grounded within the framework of the case study as well as computationally sound.

Truth tables also point to patterns in case and factor selection. Note that there is no variation among cases on the *Strong motivation* factor—all cases have a positive value. As information analysis will show, this variable will not be informative about the dependent variable since its presence in all cases does not help differentiate among the outcomes. Moreover, the two unambiguously successful cases in Table 4.3, Laos and Cuba, have positive values for most of the independent variables. This does not help us understand the importance of the individual factors, many of which are also present in the ambiguous or unsuccessful cases. This example suggests that the results might be highly dependent on certain cases or a subset of the variables, requiring further analytic tools to examine such potential dependence.

These are features of the underlying data, and information analysis works with the given data compiled by the qualitative studies. A visual scan of truth tables is already helpful in discovering such features and is a good place to start diagnostics, but it is not systematic enough, especially in relatively larger data sets, and so we proceed toward more sophisticated information analytics, which will be more revealing.

Specifically, our method examines how information about the variation in the presence or absence of the factors across the cases reduces outcome uncertainty. The choice of factors and cases should be consistent with the underlying theory-driven research design of the comparative case study. Because information analysis seeks to understand how variation in the presence or absence of factors across the set of cases relates to the variation in case outcomes, there is no point in selecting factors that do not vary across the cases or selecting only cases with the same outcome. The more variation in the data set, the more informative entropy analytics could be in reducing the uncertainty about the outcome.

Once the data tables are set up, the next few steps are basically mechanical until we get to understanding and interpreting results. The intermediate steps are also themselves informative as they reveal further features of the data and indicate patterns for close analysis and careful interpretation. The counts and calculations can be done by hand or using the Excel or R tools as discussed in the Appendixes.

Count: Calculating the Probabilities

Principles and Formulas

Count the number of times each of the outcome and factor values occur together to estimate conditional probabilities based on factor and outcome frequency counts. A joint occurrence of particular values of a factor X and outcome Y is written (x, y).

As introduced in Chapter 2, a binary system has four possibilities:

$$x = 1, y = 1$$
$$x = 0, y = 1$$
$$x = 1, y = 0$$
$$x = 0, y = 0$$

We count the number of times each of these possibilities occurs in a given set of cases and use these frequency counts for probability calculations. Conditional probability of outcome y given the value of factor x_i is calculated by dividing the joint probability that both values co-occur by the probability that this factor occurs at all, for all possible combinations (Chapter 2 explained the basic concepts applied here step by step):

1. Count the number of each of the outcomes in the given set of n cases:

$$\text{count}(y = 1)$$

$$\text{count}(y = 0) = n - \text{count}(y = 1)$$

The latter can also simply be found by subtracting the success outcome count from the total number of cases since we coded the outcomes into only two possible mutually exclusive categories.

2. Calculate total probability for each outcome state, written $p(y)$, as a fraction of the total number of cases, n:

$$p(y) = \text{count}(y)/n$$

$$p(y = 1) = \text{count}(y = 1)/n$$

$$p(y = 0) = \text{count}(y = 0)/n = 1 - p(y = 1)$$

We can find the latter by simply subtracting the probability of success outcome from 1 since the outcomes are complementary and their probability adds up to 1.

3. Count factor and outcome co-occurrence for each combination:

$$\text{count}(x_i = 1, y = 1)$$

$$\text{count}(x_i = 0, y = 1)$$

$$\text{count}(x_i = 1, y = 0)$$

$$\text{count}(x_i = 0, y = 0)$$

4. Calculate total probabilities for each factor, written $p(x)$, as a fraction of the total number of cases, n, the same way as we did for each outcome probability above:

$$p(x) = \text{count}(x)/n$$

$$p(x_i = 1) = \text{count}(x_i = 1)/n$$

$$p(x_i = 0) = \text{count}(x_i = 0)/n = 1 - \text{count}(x_i = 1)/n$$

5. Calculate joint probabilities, written $p(x, y)$, for each factor and outcome combination, by dividing each count by the total number of cases, n:

$$p(x, y) = \text{count}(x, y)/n$$

$$p(x_i = 1, y = 1) = \text{count}(x_i = 1, y = 1)/n$$

$$p(x_i = 0, y = 1) = \text{count}(x_i = 0, y = 1)/n$$

$$p(x_i = 1, y = 0) = \text{count}(x_i = 1, y = 0)/n$$

$$p(x_i = 0, y = 0) = \text{count}(x_i = 0, y = 0)/n$$

These four joint probabilities are all we need for our information calculations using the simplified *abcd* method. But, for completeness, we will also cover the conditional probabilities so that we can demonstrate the full method.

6. Calculate conditional probabilities, written $p(y|x)$, for each factor by dividing each joint probability by each factor probability:

$$p(y|x) = p(x, y)/p(x)$$

$$p(y = 1 \mid x_i = 1) = p(x_i = 1, y = 1)/p(x_i = 1)$$

$$p(y = 1 \mid x_i = 0) = p(x_i = 0, y = 1)/p(x_i = 0)$$

$$p(y = 0 \mid x_i = 1) = p(x_i = 1, y = 0)/p(x_i = 1)$$

$$p(y = 0 \mid x_i = 0) = p(x_i = 0, y = 0)/p(x_i = 0)$$

Example: Counting the Limits of Coercive Diplomacy

Perform each of the numbered tasks earlier using the Table 4.4 data.

1. Count the number of each of the outcomes in the given set of *n* cases as shown in Table 4.5.

Table 4.5 Counting Outcomes Y

Total number of cases *n*	7
Total number of Success outcomes (*y* = 1)	3
Total number of Other outcomes (*y* = 0)	4

2. Calculate outcome probabilities, written $p(y)$, as a fraction of the total number of cases, *n*, as shown in Table 4.6.

Table 4.6 Calculating Outcome Y Probabilities

Probability of Success outcome $p(y = 1) = \text{count}(y = 1)/n = 3/7$	0.43
Probability of Other outcome $p(y = 0) = 1 - 0.43$	0.57

3. Count factor and outcome co-occurrence for each combination as shown in Table 4.7.

Table 4.7 Counting the X and Y Combinations

FACTORS Independent Variables X		Data Counts: (x_i, y)			
		Count $(x_i = 1, y = 1)$	Count $(x_i = 0, y = 1)$	Count $(x_i = 1, y = 0)$	Count $(x_i = 0, y = 0)$
x_1	Clarity of objective	2	1	2	2
x_2	Strong motivation	3	0	4	0
x_3	Asymmetry of motivation	2	1	0	4
x_4	Sense of urgency	2	1	1	3
x_5	Strong leadership	3	0	3	1
x_6	Domestic support	1	2	3	1
x_7	International support	2	1	1	3
x_8	Fear of unacceptable escalation	2	1	1	3
x_9	Clarity of terms	2	1	0	4

Note that these counts reveal several missing combinations of factor and outcome values in the data, indicated by cells with counts of zero. These zeros will need to be addressed in further analytic steps. For computing information metrics, it is best to avoid missing combinations; where they are unavoidable, we will have to use a computational workaround (as in Table 4.9). Substantively, it may not be possible or theoretically justified to avoid such missing combinations given a study's set of cases and factors. Researchers should explicitly evaluate such data sets for potential implications at all stages, from research design through conclusions and interpretations.

A research design that contains at least one of each of all possible X and Y combinations would be preferable in terms of calculations and the potential information to be gained. However, the set of cases and factors should be ultimately driven by the study's objectives and theoretical framing. In the real world, some combinations may not exist or may not be practically observable. Thus, it may not be possible to avoid some missing combinations. It will be important to appropriately account for the missing combinations in subsequent steps.

4. Calculate total probabilities for each factor based on the data in Table 4.4. That table already shows frequencies, which are the empirical probabilities of a positive occurrence of each factor in the study's set of cases. We illustrate the calculation on x_1; all the variables are calculated the same way, and Table 4.8 shows the rest of the results. For presentation clarity, we switched the order by calculating $p(x_1 = 0)$ first and then finding the complementary $p(x_1 = 1)$ by subtraction, since subsequent calculations will require stringing several such terms together, and by convention, it is easier to start with zero terms. The counts are straightforward. For example, for factor x_1, *Clarity of objective*, $x_1 = 0$ in three of the seven cases, Vietnam, Libya, and Nicaragua; thus,

$$p(x_1 = 0) = \text{count}(x_1 = 0)/n = 3/7 = 0.43$$
$$p(x_1 = 1) = 1 - p(x_1 = 0) = 1 - 0.43 = 0.57$$

Table 4.8   Total Probabilities for Factors X

FACTORS Independent Variables X		Total Probability for Each Factor $p(x)$	
		$p(x_i = 0) =$ $\text{count}(x_i = 0)/n$	$p(x_i = 1) =$ $1 - p(x_i = 0)$
x_1	Clarity of objective	0.43	0.57
x_2	Strong motivation	0.00	1.00
x_3	Asymmetry of motivation	0.71	0.29
x_4	Sense of urgency	0.57	0.43
x_5	Strong leadership	0.14	0.86
x_6	Domestic support	0.43	0.57
x_7	International support	0.57	0.43
x_8	Fear of unacceptable escalation	0.57	0.43
x_9	Clarity of terms	0.71	0.29

5. Calculate joint probabilities, written $p(x, y)$, for each factor and outcome combination by dividing each count in Table 4.7 by the total number of cases, $n = 7$. Table 4.9 shows all the results; the calculations are done as follows, again on the example of x_1:

$$p(x_1 = 1, y = 1) = \text{count}(x_1 = 1, y = 1)/n = 2/7 = 0.29$$
$$p(x_1 = 0, y = 1) = \text{count}(x_1 = 0, y = 1)/n = 1/7 = 0.14$$

$$p(x_1 = 1, y = 0) = \text{count}(x_1 = 1, y = 0)/n = 2/7 = 0.29$$

$$p(x_1 = 0, y = 0) = \text{count}(x_1 = 0, y = 0)/n = 2/7 = 0.29$$

Table 4.9 Joint Probabilities for X and Y Combinations

FACTORS Independent Variables X		Joint Probability $p(x, y) = \text{count}(x, y)/n$			
		$p(x_i = 1, y = 1)$	$p(x_i = 0, y = 1)$	$p(x_i = 1, y = 0)$	$p(x_i = 0, y = 0)$
x_1	Clarity of objective	0.29	0.14	0.29	0.29
x_2	Strong motivation	0.43	0.00* (0.00001)	0.57	0.00* (0.00001)
x_3	Asymmetry of motivation	0.29	0.14	0.00* (0.00001)	0.57
x_4	Sense of urgency	0.29	0.14	0.14	0.43
x_5	Strong leadership	0.43	0.00* (0.00001)	0.43	0.14
x_6	Domestic support	0.14	0.29	0.43	0.14
x_7	International support	0.29	0.14	0.14	0.43
x_8	Fear of unacceptable escalation	0.29	0.14	0.14	0.43
x_9	Clarity of terms	0.29	0.14	0.00* (0.00001)	0.57

As a result of missing X and Y combinations in the underlying data shown in Table 4.7, there are several joint probabilities of zero (in the cells indicated by an asterisk). This must be addressed when calculating the entropy metrics using logarithms as introduced in Chapter 2 and explained more in the "Compute" step later. To ensure that logarithms are defined and to avoid division by zero, a very small value such as 0.00001 (negligible on the scale of our calculations) is substituted for the pure zero values to produce computable and meaningful results. (Note that in some of the rows the probabilities may appear not to add up to 1 due to rounding.)

6. Calculate conditional probabilities, written $p(y|x)$, for each factor by dividing each joint probability listed in Table 4.9 by the total probability for each factor listed in Table 4.8. Chapter 2 introduced the underlying concepts; here we exemplify the calculation on x_1 and show all of the results in Table 4.10.

$$p(y = 1 \mid x_1 = 1) = p(x_1 = 1, y = 1)/p(x_1 = 1) = 0.29/0.57 = 0.50$$

$$p(y = 1 \mid x_1 = 0) = p(x_1 = 0, y = 1)/p(x_1 = 0) = 0.14/0.43 = 0.33$$

$$p(y = 0 \mid x_1 = 1) = p(x_1 = 1, y = 0)/p(x_1 = 1) = 0.29/0.57 = 0.50$$

$$p(y = 0 \mid x_1 = 0) = p(x_1 = 0, y = 0)/p(x_1 = 0) = 0.29/0.43 = 0.67$$

Table 4.10   Conditional Probabilities for X and Y Combinations

FACTORS Independent Variables X		Conditional Probability $p(y\|x) = p(x, y)/p(x)$			
		$p(y = 0 \mid x_i = 0)$	$p(y = 0 \mid x_i = 1)$	$p(y = 1 \mid x_i = 0)$	$p(y = 1 \mid x_i = 1)$
x_1	Clarity of objective	0.67	0.50	0.33	0.50
x_2	Strong motivation	1.00	0.57	1.00	0.43
x_3	Asymmetry of motivation	0.80	0.00	0.20	1.00
x_4	Sense of urgency	0.75	0.33	0.25	0.67
x_5	Strong leadership	1.00	0.50	0.00	0.50
x_6	Domestic support	0.33	0.75	0.67	0.25
x_7	International support	0.75	0.33	0.25	0.67
x_8	Fear of unacceptable escalation	0.75	0.33	0.25	0.67
x_9	Clarity of terms	0.80	0.00	0.20	1.00

The conditional probability numbers are shown to two decimals rounded such that the total probability for each factor across both complementary conditions adds up to 1 as it should.

These count-based probabilities form the basis for computing the uncertainty measures.

Compute: Computing the Uncertainty Measures

Principles and Formulas

Plug the count-based probabilities into the formulas for information entropy, conditional information entropy, and mutual information to compute the uncertainty measures introduced in Chapter 2.

As Chapter 2 explained, the probability of joint events could be translated from a multiplicative to a more intuitive additive measure through the use of logarithms. Adding up the logarithmic measures would produce a simple concave function that shows maximum uncertainty where the probability of the outcome is 0.5 (a 50/50 chance) and minimum uncertainty where the probability of the outcome is either 1 or 0. The base of the logarithm corresponds to the units in which the uncertainty would be expressed; information calculations use a base 2 logarithm. It was this approach that paved the way for the binary encoding of complex information as well as measuring information quantities in bits, which are the basic units of information.

For our purposes in understanding the contributions of a given factor to knowledge about an outcome, the uncertainty measure varies from 0 when the independent variable perfectly co-occurs with the dependent variable and rises as a concave function at a decreasing rate as joint occurrences decline (Figure 2.1).

Next, continuing the use of the notation where X means a factor (independent variable) theorized to be related to the outcome Y (dependent variable), we provide the straightforward formulas for computing:

1. *Uncertainty (information entropy)* measures the uncertainty of Y, written $H(Y)$. Conceptually, this is the uncertainty associated with the outcome in the absence of the knowledge of factors. This is the total uncertainty we seek to reduce by finding whether observing the Xs could be informative toward a better understanding of Y.

$$H(Y = y) = -p(y = 1) \log_2 p(y = 1) - p(y = 0) \log_2 p(y = 0)$$

In the binary case the probabilities that $y = 0$ and that $y = 1$ are complementary; that is, they sum to 1.

$$p(y = 0) = 1 - p(y = 1)$$

We can therefore also rewrite $H(Y)$ entirely in terms of $p(y = 1)$:

$$H(Y = y) = -p(y = 1) \log_2 p(y = 1) - (1 - p(y = 1)) \log_2 (1 - p(y = 1))$$

2. *Conditional uncertainty (conditional information entropy)* measures the uncertainty of Y given knowledge of X, written $H(Y|X)$. This is a transitional step that allows us to systematically evaluate the level of uncertainty in Y given that we know the condition of X—namely, whether each X factor is present or not.

$$
\begin{aligned}
H(Y = y \mid X = x_i) = &-p(x_i = 0) \, [p(y = 0 \mid x_i = 0) \log_2 p(y = 0 \mid x_i = 0) \\
&+ p(y = 1 \mid x_i = 0) \log_2 p(y = 1 \mid x_i = 0)] \\
&- p(x_i = 1) \, [p(y = 0 \mid x_i = 1) \log_2 p(y = 0 \mid x_i = 1) \\
&+ p(y = 1 \mid x_i = 1) \log_2 p(y = 1 \mid x_i = 1)]
\end{aligned}
$$

The underlying conditional probabilities were already calculated in previous steps, so they just need to be plugged into this equation to compute the conditional entropy.

3. *Uncertainty reduction or information gain (mutual information)* measures the reduced uncertainty in Y due to the knowledge of X, written $I(Y; X)$. It means the difference between entropy (uncertainty about the outcome in the absence of any additional information) and conditional entropy (uncertainty about the outcome given that we know whether a factor is present or not) as explained in Chapter 2:

$$I(Y; X) = H(Y) - H(Y|X)$$

$$= I(Y = y; X = x_i)$$

$$= H(Y = y) - H(Y = y \mid X = x_i)$$

Conditional entropy and mutual information can be calculated in more complex ways based on combinations of several independent variables at a time as well as in terms of sequences of variables or other combinatorics. However, we introduce the method using simple binary calculations with our purpose in mind of providing simple but useful tools for qualitative scholars. By mastering these basics, one can always add complexity using the same underlying approach.

Example: Computing the Limits of Coercive Diplomacy

To compute the uncertainty measures, plug the probabilities found in the "Count" step into the formulas for information entropy, conditional information entropy, and mutual information. Again, the computations are exemplified in the following; all can be done by hand or automated using the Excel or R tools explained in Appendixes A and B, respectively.

1. *Uncertainty (information entropy)* of Y is computed by plugging the outcome probabilities from Table 4.6 into the information entropy formula as shown here:

$$H(Y = y) = -p(y = 1) \log_2 p(y = 1) - p(y = 0) \log_2 p(y = 0)$$

$$= -0.43 \log_2 0.43 - 0.57 \log_2 0.57$$

$$= 0.985$$

2. *Conditional uncertainty (conditional information entropy)* is computed by plugging the total probabilities from Table 4.8 and the conditional probabilities

from Table 4.10 into the conditional information entropy formula. The detailed computation is demonstrated on the example of x_1; all the variables are computed the same way with all the results reported in Table 4.11.

$$H(Y=y \mid X=x_1) = -\,p(x_1=0)\,[p(y=0 \mid x_1=0)\,\log_2 p(y=0 \mid x_1=0)$$
$$+\,p(y=1 \mid x_1=0)\,\log_2 p(y=1 \mid x_1=0)]$$
$$-\,p(x_1=1)\,[p(y=0 \mid x_1=1)\,\log_2 p(y=0 \mid x_1=1)$$
$$+\,p(y=1 \mid x_1=1)\,\log_2 p(y=1 \mid x_1=1)]$$
$$=-\,0.43\,[0.67\,\log_2 0.67 + 0.33\,\log_2 0.33]$$
$$-\,0.57\,[0.50\,\log_2 0.50 + 0.50\,\log_2 0.50]$$
$$=0.965$$

Table 4.11   Conditional Uncertainty of Outcome Y Due to Each Factor X Measured by Conditional Information Entropy

FACTORS Independent Variables X		Conditional Information Entropy H(Y|X)
x_1	Clarity of objective	0.96
x_2	Strong motivation	0.99
x_3	Asymmetry of motivation	0.52
x_4	Sense of urgency	0.86
x_5	Strong leadership	0.86
x_6	Domestic support	0.86
x_7	International support	0.86
x_8	Fear of unacceptable escalation	0.86
x_9	Clarity of terms	0.52

This table shows the outcome uncertainty conditional on the knowledge of each factor (the frequency and patterns of whether it is present or not across the cases), rounded to show two decimals. A larger number means more uncertainty.

3. *Uncertainty reduction or information gain (mutual information)* is computed by plugging the outcome uncertainty measure $H(Y=y)$ and conditional uncertainty measures from Table 4.11 into the mutual information formula for each factor. Again, the detailed computation is demonstrated on the example of x_1; all the variables are computed the same way with all the results reported in Table 4.12.

$$I(Y = y; X = x_1) = H(Y = y) - H(Y = y|X = x_1)$$
$$= 0.985 - 0.965$$
$$= 0.02$$

4. Finally, the *direction* of the relationship needs to be assessed to determine whether the presence of X is associated with the presence or the absence of Y. If the former, we label the direction positive; if the latter, we label it negative. Direction will often be obvious from visual inspection, but we can check it objectively with the following formula. If it evaluates greater than zero, then the relationship is positive. If it evaluates less than zero, then the relationship is negative.

$$Direction = [count(Y = 1, X = 1) + count(Y = 0, X = 0)]$$
$$- [count(Y = 0, X = 1) + count(Y = 1, X = 0)]$$

Conceptually, you can see that this is just comparing the two diagonals in a 2 × 2 table. If the main diagonal, where X and Y take the same value, is larger than the second diagonal, where X and Y take different values, then the direction of the relationship will be positive. If the opposite obtains, the direction of the relationship will be negative.

Table 4.12 Information Gain or the Uncertainty Reduction in Outcome Y Due to Factor X Measured by Mutual Information

FACTORS Independent Variables X		Mutual Information $I(Y; X) = H(Y) - H(Y|X)$	Direction
x_1	Clarity of objective	0.02	Positive
x_2	Strong motivation	0.00	Positive
x_3	Asymmetry of motivation	0.47	Positive
x_4	Sense of urgency	0.13	Positive
x_5	Strong leadership	0.13	Positive
x_6	Domestic support	0.13	Negative
x_7	International support	0.13	Positive
x_8	Fear of unacceptable escalation	0.13	Positive
x_9	Clarity of terms	0.47	Positive

This table shows information gain due to each factor. A larger number indicates a more informative factor, meaning that we achieve a greater reduction in uncertainty or, in other words, greater information gain about the expected outcome status from knowing whether the factor is present or not (in terms of frequency and patterns across the cases). The most informative factors are shaded. The numerical results also enable objective comparison, ranking, and prioritization of the factors in terms of their relative information value, direction of the relationships, and the magnitude of information gain that each produces.

The notion of a 2 × 2 representation of the relationship between two variables also provides the key for our shortcut method for doing the information theory calculations.

Calculate: A Shortcut

Table 4.13 Joint Probabilities

	X = 1	X = 0
Y = 1	a	b
Y = 0	c	d

Instead of going through all of the probability calculations, we can jump directly from a 2 × 2 joint probability table to the information metric calculations. The 2 × 2 joint probability table shows the relative frequency of each combination of possible values for the outcome variable and an independent (explanatory) factor. For expressing these new formulas, we will use a labeling system in which the percentage of cases where both X = 1 and Y = 1 is labeled a, the percentage of X = 0 and Y = 1 is b, the percentage where X = 1 and Y = 0 is c, and the percentage where both X and Y are zero is labeled d. Because of these labels, we call this the *abcd* method. Table 4.13 shows the labeling system. Each of the cells represents the number of occurrences of the specific combination divided by the total number of cases (the joint probabilities).

We have already calculated these probabilities for *The Limits of Coercive Diplomacy* example as displayed in Table 4.9. From there, the conditional entropy, mutual information, and relationship direction can be quickly calculated with the following three formulas (as presented in Chapter 2):

Information entropy

$$H(Y) = - (a + b) \log_2 (a + b) - (c + d) \log_2 (c + d)$$

Conditional entropy

$$H(Y|X) = - [d (\log_2 (d) - \log_2 (b + d)) + b (\log_2 (b) - \log_2 (b + d))]$$
$$- [c (\log_2 (c) - \log_2 (a + c)) + a (\log_2 (a) - \log_2 (a + c))]$$

Mutual information

$$I(Y; X) = H(Y) - H(Y|X)$$

Direction

$$Direction = (a + d) - (b + c)$$

As we show in the Appendixes, these formulas are straightforward to implement in a spreadsheet program such as Microsoft Excel or in the statistical program R. Applying them to the *abcd* values from Table 4.9 produces the same value for information entropy $H(Y) = 0.985$ and the same values for mutual information and direction as in Tables 4.11 and 4.12.

Compare: Understanding the Outcomes

Principles and Meaning

The results provided by information analysis are quantitative measures of uncertainty and leverage. We can understand the information effects of each independent variable in terms of the reduction in our uncertainty about the value of the dependent variable, the outcome that the comparative case studies seek to explain.

$H(Y)$ measures how uncertain we are whether the outcome will be successful in the absence of knowledge about the explanatory factors. It is based on our empirical frequency-based observations and counts of outcomes in the known cases. In the world of few observations represented by the in-depth but small-n comparative case studies, this uncertainty may be vast. Thus, it is useful to select those factors that would most reduce this uncertainty.

For each factor, $H(Y|X)$ measures how uncertain we are about whether the case will be a success given that we know whether the factor is present or not. $I(Y; X)$ then measures mutual information—the reduction in outcome uncertainty or information gain—from knowing each factor. When mutual information is close to zero, it means that the theorized factor tells us nearly nothing about the likely outcome. There is no significant reduction in uncertainty about the value of Y from knowing the value of X. When mutual information is close to the original uncertainty value of $H(Y)$, it means that the factor almost perfectly predicts the outcome. Uncertainty about the value of Y essentially disappears when we know the value of X. The magnitude of the mutual information score for the different factors provides a numerical scale for making a systematic comparison indicating the relative contribution of each factor to reducing uncertainty about the outcome.

Sets of numerical results (such as Table 4.12) enable us to rank the qualitative case factors and evaluate their relative as well as cumulative impact. The information method provides quantitative answers about the magnitude of uncertainty about the outcome, as well as meaningful quantitative ranking of how much we can learn about this uncertain outcome given each observed factor that is theorized to be related to the outcome. From the relative impacts, we can conclude which factors are most useful to know to reduce the outcome uncertainty. This is helpful in research for discerning the leverage from each independent variable. And it may be especially useful in practical decision making. When constrained by limited resources, managers or policy makers must prioritize what factors must be ascertained to gain the most insight into a decision concerning an uncertain but consequential or costly outcome. We can also begin to discern the impact of individual cases on the analytic conclusions, the subject addressed in more depth in Chapter 6 on sensitivity analysis. Overall, the answers offer actionable information pertinent to research and practice.

We can now look more closely at the additional analytic leverage provided by the information metrics in our *Coercive Diplomacy* (1994) example. But first, in Figure 4.1, we provide a summary of the four steps for implementing the information method.

STEP 1: QUANTIFY
Set Up a Truth Table for Comparative Case Analysis

Create a data matrix with the cases on one dimension and the factors and outcomes on the other to account for every possible combination of values for each of the Xs and Y. All values must be binary {0,1} where 1 means a factor is present, otherwise 0.

STEP 2: COUNT
Count Occurrences and
Calculate the Joint Probabilities

2.1 Count factor and outcome *co-occurrence* for each of the combinations of X and Y values.

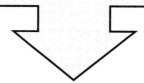

$$\text{count}(x_i = 1, y = 1) \qquad \text{count}(x_i = 0, y = 1)$$
$$\text{count}(x_i = 1, y = 0) \qquad \text{count}(x_i = 0, y = 0)$$

2.2 Calculate the *joint probabilities* for each factor and outcome combination by dividing the co-occurrence counts by the total number of cases (n),

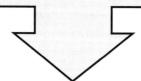

$$a = \text{count}(x_i = 1, y = 1)/n \qquad b = \text{count}(x_i = 0, y = 1)/n$$
$$c = \text{count}(x_i = 1, y = 0)/n \qquad d = \text{count}(x_i = 0, y = 0)/n$$

STEP 3: COMPUTE
Compute the Uncertainty Measures

3.1 Compute Total Uncertainty (Information Entropy) for Y.

$$H(Y) = -(a + b) \log_2 (a + b) - (c + d) \log_2 (c + d)$$

3.2 Compute Conditional Uncertainty of Y given each X.

$$H(Y|X) = -[d (\log_2 (d) - \log_2 (b + d)) + b (\log_2 (b) - \log_2 (b + d))]$$
$$- [c (\log_2 (c) - \log_2 (a + c)) + a (\log_2 (a) - \log_2 (a + c))]$$

3.3 Compute Uncertainty Reduction (Mutual Information) for each X.

$$I(Y; X) = H(Y) - H(Y|X)$$

3.4 Note whether the relationship is positive or negative.

$$Direction = (a + d) - (b + c)$$

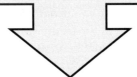

STEP 4: COMPARE
Understand the Outcomes

The information calculations produce a simple metric of the degree to which knowledge of the value of each X is informative about the value of Y for the particular set of comparative cases under analysis.

Comparing and ranking the information scores is a systematic, rigorous, and replicable way to identify the most and least informative factors.

This figure shows the four steps of the information method using the shortcut abcd *approach for the calculations. The objective and comparable information metrics enable a systematic interpretation of the qualitative comparative case study findings.*

Figure 4.1 Implementing the Information Method: Quantify, Count, Compute, and Compare

Example: Comparing the Limits of Coercive Diplomacy

As shown in Table 4.12, the mutual information values in *The Limits of Coercive Diplomacy* fall into three ranges, indicating factors that are—in relative magnitude—most, least, and somewhat informative about the outcome.

First, *Asymmetry of motivation* and *Clarity of terms* are the only variables that provide significant predictive leverage. Both have a mutual information score of 0.47. This uncertainty reduction suggests that knowledge of either of these two factors can account for nearly 50% of the expected outcome. This may be less than ideal but is still far more informative than all other factors theorized to be important enough based on deep study of the discipline of international affairs and the cases of the phenomena in question chosen by the authors.

Second, we learn from this analysis that the *Clarity of objective* and *Strong motivation* variables tell us essentially nothing about whether or not coercive diplomacy is likely to succeed (mutual information is nearly zero). It is no surprise that *Strong motivation* provides no information gain. As we saw in the truth table (Table 4.3), strong motivation is present in every case: It cannot help us discriminate between success and failure. Future research designs may take this into account upfront when building theory and selecting factors and cases. *Clarity of objective* is also noninformative. In this instance, that is because the pattern for the variable clearly has no connection to the outcome pattern: This factor is present in two of the successful cases and two of the failure cases and is absent in two failures and one success. The resulting information metric is the same as for the *Strong motivation* variable: Neither variable provides information to discriminate between successful and nonsuccessful outcomes.

Third, for the other variables (*Sense of urgency, Strong leadership, Domestic support, International support,* and *Fear of unacceptable escalation*), the mutual information measure is very low at 0.13. This means that knowing about any of these variables can only reduce the total uncertainty by around 13%. Reviewing the earlier information method steps, we can see that each of these variables shows a different pattern, but none matches up systematically with the pattern of outcome successes and failures.

Overall, the findings provide objective and comparable measures to inform interpretation of the results. The finding of two most informative variables is very important in the realm of complex and highly consequential international diplomacy. The contribution of the other variables is relatively scant. The information-theoretic method enables systematically sorting out these degrees of knowledge gain to inform qualitative interpretations. Researchers and practitioners alike can strongly benefit from better understanding these factors as well as incorporating other findings into future research and policy designs.

A complex and policy-relevant subject matter such as this also warrants further investigation into the residual uncertainty and the sensitivity of the results to various aspects of research design identified in Chapter 3. *The Limits of Coercive Diplomacy* (George & Simons, 1994) illustrates how information-theoretic results can help us understand the relative impact of individual cases. For example, both of the factors found to be most informative have values that line up (positive to positive and vice versa) with all but one of the cases. That is, in the cases of Laos and Cuba, where the outcome is positive, the values for each of these variables are also positive and vice versa.

The Nicaragua case does *not* line up for both factors. A closer examination of this case reveals important implications for the findings as well as research design. The case of Nicaragua exemplifies the qualitative ambiguities in underlying case study evidence cautioned against in Chapter 3. Such challenges may account for some of the unexplained uncertainty. In this case, the coercive diplomacy objectives were defined as the removal from power of the Sandinista government. This was indeed accomplished in the February 1990 elections but only after years of coercive diplomacy efforts by the United States. The Nicaragua case study chapter discusses this outcome as part of "explaining the limits of success" (George & Simons, 1994, p. 188), and given this interpretation, the outcome is coded "Yes" in truth Table 4.2 and quantified as 1 in Table 4.3. However, George and Simons also point to the possible limits on the extent to which the outcome can be directly attributed to coercive diplomacy in the context of other forces that may have contributed to the outcome. More in-depth qualitative evidence might be necessary to sort out this outcome more precisely.

From the perspective of comparative information gain, there are only three successes in this set of cases, and ambiguities in one of them is an important area to explore for further cumulative learning, uncertainty reduction, and to assess the sensitivity of the findings. We take up the relatively more advanced issues of sensitivity analysis in Chapter 6, after demonstrating the application of the basic information method steps on several more diverse examples in Chapter 5.

Conclusion

In this chapter, we have provided a step-by-step guide to calculating information metrics for comparative case analysis. The four fundamental steps of information analytics for comparative case studies are quantify, count, compute, and compare. These methods are based on simple counts—empirical probabilities. If you can count, you can do it.

We demonstrated the information approach by reexamining a prominent structured-focused comparative case study from political science. George and Simons's (1994) landmark study on the role of military coercion in international politics had relied on the reader's subjective and visual assessment. Instead, we provided a systematic and replicable metric for understanding the relationships between the explanatory factors and the observed outcomes. These results provided a concrete example of the potential for information theory to enrich comparative case study methods.

In the next chapter, we reinforce this example and push further to demonstrate the application of the information method for enhancing comparative case studies with examples from several other fields.

Additional resources are provided at http://study.sagepub.com/drozdova.

Information Metrics at Work—Three Examples

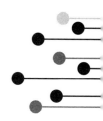

I n this chapter, we present three worked-out real-world examples of using information metrics to improve our understanding of case study analysis. The examples are taken from the fields of ecology, education, and medicine. Of course, the fundamental approach of information metrics applies to any field or problem where uncertain outcomes could be illuminated by observing some related factors. Each example here draws on the straightforward and simple techniques set out in Chapter 4 to provide these studies with a more systematic set of findings about the relative impact of each of their respective independent variables on their dependent variable outcomes. In each example, we show that information metrics can help analysts and policy makers move beyond the subjective assessment of the comparative case study results. We do the first example using the full set of probabilities. The second and third examples are worked out just using joint probabilities with the more efficient *abcd* method.

Example 1—Ecology: Information Analysis for Tropical Forest Loss

The destruction of tropical forests has become a particularly critical issue in the context of contentious policy debates on global climate change. Thomas Rudel's (2005) book on the factors contributing to tropical forest loss is an excellent example of a meta-analysis combining a number of regional studies of forest loss. Rudel's goal is to synthesize these local studies to develop a global understanding of the forces that contribute to forest loss.

Quantify: Setting up a Truth Table

Rudel's (2005) global analysis is based on synthesizing multiple studies by region and then using qualitative comparative analysis (QCA) to look for patterns of factors. We address QCA and its relationship with information theory in Chapter 7. At this point, we just want to show how information theory can improve our understanding of the impact of the individual factors identified by Rudel. Rudel's analysis is built on a large number of truth tables summarizing the literature on forest loss by region. Most of this work is implied but not included explicitly in the book. Rudel does, however, provide an example of the analysis process for eight studies of tropical forest loss in Ecuador. Table 5.1 displays the truth table values for Rudel's Ecuador example.

The question we want to answer is, How much does the variation in each of the independent variables tell us about the variation in the dependent variable (*Forest loss*)? Table 5.1 includes the outcome variable (*Forest loss*) but, as with the studies we examined in Chapter 4, interpretation of the relationships is largely left to the subjective assessment of the reader. Information theory can provide us with a systematic and reproducible understanding of how much knowledge of the independent variables contributes to knowledge of the outcome.

As set out in Chapter 4, we can measure this relationship in terms of information. We do this with our four steps: quantify, count, compute, and compare. The quantification has already been done by Rudel (2005). We have a clear table of dichotomous variable values and a dichotomous outcome variable, as shown in Table 5.1.

Count: Calculating the Probabilities

The counting step begins with identifying how many times each of the possible combinations of the independent and dependent variable values occurs for each of

Table 5.1   Truth Table for Rudel (2005) Data on Tropical Forest Cover in Ecuador

	Data Era	Smallholder Agriculture	Mineral Extraction	Logging in Region	Road Building	Colonization Program	Forest Loss (Y)
Echevarria	1980s	0	1	0	0	0	0
Rudel	1980s	1	0	0	1	1	1
Pichon	1980s	1	1	0	1	1	1
Hiroaka	1970s	1	1	0	0	1	1
Becker	1990s	1	0	0	0	0	1
Sierra	1990s	1	1	1	1	0	1
Wunder	1990s	1	0	1	1	0	1
Rudel/Bates	1990s	1	0	1	0	0	0
"1" frequency		0.88	0.50	0.38	0.50	0.38	0.75

Data from Rudel (2005, p. 27).

the independent variables. These possible combinations are simply the four following scenarios:

$$x = 1 \text{ and } y = 1$$
$$x = 0 \text{ and } y = 1$$
$$x = 1 \text{ and } y = 0$$
$$x = 0 \text{ and } y = 0$$

Table 5.2 shows the counts for each of these combinations. This would be easy enough to do by hand, or, as we demonstrate in Appendixes A and B, you can get Excel or R, respectively, to do it for you. (These worked-out examples can also be downloaded in either the Excel or R version from http://study.sagepub.com/drozdova.) The first row, for example, shows that there is only one instance where smallholder agriculture is absent and that there is no forest loss. There is likewise only one case that finds smallholder agriculture present and no forest loss. There are no cases where smallholder agriculture is absent and forest loss is present. And there are six cases where smallholder agriculture is present and forest loss is present.

To construct our probabilities, we need a few other counts here as well. These are equally trivial and are shown in Table 5.3.

Table 5.2 Counting the X and Y Combinations

Forest Loss Conditions	Data Counts: (x, y)			
	Count $(x_i = 1, y = 1)$	Count $(x_i = 0, y = 1)$	Count $(x_i = 1, y = 0)$	Count $(x_i = 0, y = 0)$
Smallholder agriculture (x_1)	6	0	1	1
Mineral extraction (x_2)	3	3	1	1
Logging in region (x_3)	2	4	1	1
Road building (x_4)	4	2	0	2
Colonization programs (x_5)	3	3	0	2

Table 5.3 Other Quantities to Count

Total number of cases n	8
Total number of Success outcomes ($y = 1$)	6
Total number of Other outcomes ($y = 0$)	2

We can now calculate the joint probabilities. As explained in Chapter 4, these are just the probability of each outcome enumerated in Table 5.2. These are calculated simply by dividing the counts in Table 5.2 by the total number of cases, which in this study is 8. Table 5.4 shows each of these probabilities.

The one trick we need here is to substitute a very small value, such as 0.00001 for the pure zero values, to be sure that the logarithms are defined, as discussed in Chapters 2 and 4. These values are indicated in Table 5.4 with an asterisk.

The next calculation is the total probability for each possible value of the independent variables. This is just the total number of times each independent variable is 0 or 1, divided by the total number of cases (n). This means for each row in Table 5.2 adding the values from the first and third columns ($x = 1$) and those from the second and fourth columns ($x = 0$). Then divide each result by n, which is 8 in this study. So for the *Smallholder agriculture* variable, we have $(1 + 0)/8 = 0.125$ and $(1 + 6)/8 = 0.875$. Of course, it will always be the case that these two values are complements, so you could also calculate the second value (total probability that $x = 1$) by subtracting the total probability that $x = 0$ from 1. (The places where the values do

Table 5.4 Joint Probabilities

Forest Loss Conditions	Joint Probability: $p(x, y) = \text{count}(x, y)/n$			
	$p(x_i = 1, y = 1)$	$p(x_i = 0, y = 1)$	$p(x_i = 1, y = 0)$	$p(x_i = 0, y = 0)$
Smallholder agriculture (x_1)	0.75	0.00*	0.13	0.13
Mineral extraction (x_2)	0.38	0.38	0.13	0.13
Logging in region (x_3)	0.25	0.50	0.13	0.13
Road building (x_4)	0.50	0.25	0.00*	0.25
Colonization programs (x_5)	0.38	0.38	0.00*	0.25

(Note that in some of the rows the probabilities may appear not to add up to 1 due to rounding.)

not add to 1 are just an artifact of the representation in the tables that involve rounding.) You can also calculate the total probabilities directly from the joint probabilities (Table 5.4). For any given row, the values in the first and third columns add to the total probability that the variable is 1. The values in the second and fourth rows add to the total probability that the variable is 0.

We also need the total probabilities for $y = 0$ and $y = 1$. These are simple to calculate from the counts in Table 5.3. The probability that $y = 0$ is just the count of the number of times $y = 0$ divided by the total number of cases, n. For this data set, that means $2/8 = 0.25$. The total probability for $y = 1$ is $6/8 = 0.75$.

For each combination of x and y values, the conditional probability is the probability that y takes on a specific value, given a specific value of x. We need the probability that $y = 0$, given that $x = 0$; the probability that $y = 0$, given that $x = 1$; the probability that $y = 1$, given that $x = 0$; and the probability that $y = 1$, given that $x = 1$. In each case, this is the joint probability (Table 5.4) divided by the total probability (Table 5.5). For example, the conditional probability that $y = 1$ given that $x = 1$ is the probability that $x = 1$ and $y = 1$ (column 1 of Table 5.4) divided by the total probability that $x = 1$ (column 2 of Table 5.5).

The conditional probabilities are shown in Table 5.6. You can see, for example, in the third column of the first row that there is zero probability of forest loss where smallholder agriculture is not the norm. That is generated by the fact that there are no cases of forest loss ($y = 1$) and no smallholder agriculture ($x_1 = 0$). The conditional probability of forest loss, given an absence of smallholder agriculture, is zero.

Table 5.5   Total Probabilities for X Values

Forest Loss Conditions	Total Probability for Each Condition: $p(x)$	
	$p(x_i = 0)$	$p(x_i = 1)$
Smallholder agriculture (x_1)	0.12	0.88
Mineral extraction (x_2)	0.50	0.50
Logging in region (x_3)	0.63	0.37
Road building (x_4)	0.50	0.50
Colonization programs (x_5)	0.63	0.37

Table 5.6 Conditional Probabilities

Forest Loss Conditions	Conditional Probability: $p(y\|x) = p(x, y)/p(x)$			
	$p(y = 1 \| x_i = 1)$	$p(y = 1 \| x_i = 0)$	$p(y = 0 \| x_i = 1)$	$p(y = 0 \| x_i = 0)$
Smallholder agriculture (x_1)	0.86	0.00*	0.14	1.00
Mineral extraction (x_2)	0.75	0.75	0.25	0.25
Logging in region (x_3)	0.67	0.80	0.33	0.20
Road building (x_4)	1.00	0.50	0.00*	0.50
Colonization programs (x_5)	1.00	0.60	0.00*	0.40

Compute: Calculating the Information Metrics

Information entropy is a measure of the uncertainty of a random variable. When the value is known for certain, the entropy is 0. When we have no idea what the value will be, then entropy is 1. Shannon's (1948) famous entropy equation is

$$H(Y) = -\sum_{i=1}^{n} p(y) \log p(y)$$

When we are working with a dichotomous variable, we use log base 2 for this calculation. In our current example, y is coded 1 for tropical forest loss and 0 for no forest loss. Expanding Shannon's equation, we can calculate the $H(Y)$ value by adding the probability that $y = 1$ multiplied by the base 2 log of the probability that $y = 1$ to the probability that $y = 0$ multiplied by the base 2 log of the probability that $y = 0$. Drawing on the total probabilities for y that we calculated earlier gives us the following value for $H(Y)$:

$$H(Y) = -\sum_{i=1}^{n} p(y) \log_2 p(y)$$
$$= -[p(y = 0) \log_2 p(y = 0) + p(y = 1) \log_2 p(y = 1)]$$
$$= -[0.25 \log_2 (0.25) + 0.75 \log_2 (0.75)]$$
$$= -[0.25 (-2) + 0.75 (-0.415)]$$
$$= 0.811$$

We are now set to calculate the conditional information entropy. So far, everything has been exceedingly simple. The next step looks a little more complex but, as we demonstrated in Chapter 4, is really almost as straightforward computationally and conceptually as everything else we have done so far. If you can count, you can do this.

Instead of just guessing Y, which we saw was going to be hard, we want to know how much better our guess would be if we knew the value of one of the independent variables. That is, how much information about the state of the dependent variable can we derive from knowing the value of one of the independent variables.

Our metric for this quantity is the conditional value of H for each of our independent variables. Here is the conditional entropy equation:

$$H(Y|X) = -p(x=0) \, [p(y=0 \mid x=0) \log_2 p(y=0 \mid x=0)$$
$$+ \, p(y=1 \mid x=0) \log_2 p(y=1 \mid x=0)]$$
$$- \, p(x=1) \, [p(y=0 \mid x=1) \log_2 p(y=0 \mid x=1)$$
$$+ \, p(y=1 \mid x=1) \log_2 p(y=1 \mid x=1)]$$

Don't panic! We have all the values we need to fill this in from the total probability values in Table 5.5 and the conditional probability values in Table 5.6. These, combined with the ability to calculate the base 2 logarithms, will do the trick. As we show in Appendix A, Excel can make this all exceedingly straightforward.

We can see from Table 5.7 that information entropy (uncertainty) is minimized when we know the values of the *Smallholder agriculture* and the *Road building* variables. On the other hand, knowing about the presence or absence of extractable minerals tells us essentially nothing about the likelihood of forest destruction. There is no difference between the information entropy for the *Forest loss* outcome alone and the conditional information entropy when we know the value of *Mineral extraction*.

Table 5.7   Conditional Information Entropy

Forest Loss Conditions	$H(Y|X)$
Smallholder agriculture (x_1)	0.52
Mineral extraction (x_2)	0.81
Logging in region (x_3)	0.80
Road building (x_4)	0.50
Colonization programs (x_5)	0.61

This table shows the absolute amount of uncertainty we will have about the presence or absence of forest loss given that we know the value of each of the independent variables. Lower values show less uncertainty.

This brings us to our final metric, the measure of mutual information, or the reduction in uncertainty about Y due to our knowledge of X. This is simply calculated by taking the difference between the total information entropy of Y and the conditional information entropy of Y given X:

$$I(Y; X) = H(Y) - H(Y|X)$$

Table 5.8 shows the mutual information for the Rudel (2005) data set on tropical forest loss in Ecuador. Again, we can see that we learn the most about the likelihood of forest

Table 5.8 Mutual Information: The Uncertainty Reduction in Outcome Y Due to Factor X

Forest Loss Conditions	Mutual Information $I(Y; X) = H(Y) - H(Y|X)$	Direction
Smallholder agriculture (x_1)	0.29	Positive
Mineral extraction (x_2)	0.00	Negative
Logging in region (x_3)	0.02	Negative
Road building (x_4)	0.31	Positive
Colonization programs (x_5)	0.20	Positive

This table shows how much information about the presence or absence of forest loss is gained from knowing the value of each of the independent variables. Higher values show more mutual information.

loss from knowing about smallholder agriculture and road building. Each of these drops the information entropy, the uncertainty, of Y by about 0.3, which is nearly by 40% since the original uncertainty $H(Y)$ was around 0.8. In contrast, knowledge about mineral extraction adds no additional information to help us predict the likelihood of forest loss.

Table 5.8 also shows the direction of each of these effects. For each variable, the direction is calculated by taking the sum of the joint probabilities that $x = 1$ and $y = 1$ and the joint probability that $x = 0$ and $y = 0$ and subtracting from that the sum of the joint probabilities that $x = 1$ and $y = 0$ and the joint probability that $x = 0$ and $y = 1$. If this difference is positive, then the direction of the relationship is positive; that is, when X increases, we expect Y to increase. If it is negative, then when X increases, we expect Y to decrease.

The joint probability values can be retrieved from Table 5.4. In this example, we can see that all of the relationships are positive, with the exception of *Logging* and *Mineral extraction*. But both of those relationships are essentially noninformative, so the direction for those two variables carries little real meaning.

Compare: What Does It All Mean?

Now that we have generated all of these nifty metrics, it is time for the last step, to interpret what they really mean.

Rudel's (2005) excellent and extensive compilation of data on tropical forest destruction identifies the variables of interest for understanding forest loss. It uses QCA analysis to try to get at how these variables cohere across the different cases. It does not, however, offer a systematic way to understand the relative impact of the different factors. That critical step is left to subjective assessment. Our application of simple information metrics allows us to clearly identify and communicate the relative impact of each of the theoretically identified factors.

Interestingly, the exploitation of mineral and logging resources does not appear to significantly affect forest loss. The effects of *Smallholder agriculture* and of *Road building* and, to a somewhat lesser extent, the persistence of *Colonization policies* are much clearer.

There should be some valuable policy implications from knowing which of these factors has had the clearest impact on deforestation.

Example 2—Education: Accounting for Teaching Quality

Our second example comes from the field of education. One of the central challenges of educational improvement is the move from successful small-scale experiments to the widespread deployment of teaching innovations. Cynthia Coburn, Jennifer Russell, Julia Heath Kaufman, and Mary Kay Stein conducted a small-*n* qualitative study of the role of teachers' social networks in the sustainability and scalability of educational reforms (Coburn, Russell, Kaufman, & Stein, 2012).

Quantify: Setting Up a Truth Table

The authors studied 12 teachers and had 6 variables of interest. The variables measured the depth of social network connections, the expertise of the teachers, and the strength of network ties. These factors were measured over the course of 2 years, so the three characteristics— depth, expertise, and tie strength—are each assessed at two different time points. The authors converted all of their findings to dichotomous {0, 1} measures. The resulting data are displayed in Table 5.9.

Again, we want to know how much we can learn about the dependent variable (*High-quality instruction in the third year*) by knowing about the independent variables. For this example, we are going to use the shortcut *abcd* method, which calculates the information metrics directly from the joint probabilities. The quantification has already been done by Coburn et al. (2012) so we can move right to the counting.

Table 5.9 Truth Table for Coburn et al. (2012) Data on Teacher Networks

	Depth—Year 1	Expertise—Year 1	Tie Strength—Year 1	Depth—Year 2	Expertise—Year 2	Tie Strength—Year 2	High-Quality Instruction—Year 2	Outcome—High-Quality Instruction—Year 3
Denise	0	1	0	1	1	1	1	1
Nina	0	0	0	1	1	1	1	1
Sarah	0	0	1	0	1	0	1	0
Tara	0	1	0	0	0	1	0	0
Larissa	0	1	0	1	0	0	1	0
Winona	0	1	1	0	0	1	1	0
Kathy	0	1	1	1	0	0	1	1
Laura	0	1	1	1	1	0	1	1
Don	1	0	0	1	0	1	0	0
Quinn	1	0	1	1	1	1	1	1
Florence	1	1	1	0	1	0	0	1

Data from Coburn et al. (2012, p. 155).

Count: Calculating the Probabilities

To generate the joint probabilities for the *abcd* method, we first need to count the number of occurrences of each of the *x* and *y* combinations: $x = 0$ and $y = 0$, $x = 1$ and $y = 0$, $x = 0$ and $y = 1$, and $x = 1$ and $y = 1$. This data set has seven independent variables, so this will be 28 cells as in Table 5.10.

We will also need our counts of the values taken by the dependent variable, which are shown in Table 5.11.

We can now calculate the joint probabilities. We divide the counts in each cell of Table 5.10 by the total number of cases (11). Table 5.12 displays the results along with the *abcd* labels we will use for the calculation of the information metrics.

Table 5.10 Counting the X and Y Combinations

High-Quality Instruction Conditions	Data Counts: (x, y)			
	Count $(x_i = 1, y = 1)$	Count $(x_i = 0, y = 1)$	Count $(x_i = 1, y = 0)$	Count $(x_i = 0, y = 0)$
Depth—Year 1 (x_1)	2	4	1	4
Expertise—Year 1 (x_2)	4	2	3	2
Tie strength—Year 1 (x_3)	4	2	2	3
Depth—Year 2 (x_4)	5	1	2	3
Expertise—Year 2 (x_5)	5	1	1	4
Tie strength—Year 2 (x_6)	3	3	3	2
High-quality instruction—Year 2 (x_7)	5	1	3	2

Unlike the previous example, there are no zero cells, so we don't need to worry about adjusting those values.

Compute: Calculating the Information Metrics

With six successes out of eleven trials, the overall outcome uncertainty in this study will be very high. In the study of forest loss in Ecuador, there were seven cases of high forest loss out of nine cases. That meant that you could just always guess that there would be forest loss and you would be right seven times out of nine. That will not be the case in this example. We can calculate the total information entropy of Y from the *abcd* values. There are different *abcd* values for each independent variable X, but the total information entropy of the outcome will be the same for each X. This means we can use any of the *abcd* combinations to

Table 5.11 Other Quantities to Count

Total number of cases *n*	11
Total number of Success outcomes $(y = 1)$	6
Total number of Other outcomes $(y = 0)$	5

Table 5.12 Joint Probabilities

	Joint Probability: $p(x, y) = count(x, y)/n$			
	$p(x_i = 1, y = 1)$	$p(x_i = 0, y = 1)$	$p(x_i = 1, y = 0)$	$p(x_i = 0, y = 0)$
High-Quality Instruction Conditions	a	b	c	d
Depth—Year 1 (x_1)	0.18	0.36	0.09	0.36
Expertise—Year 1 (x_2)	0.36	0.18	0.27	0.18
Tie strength—Year 1 (x_3)	0.36	0.18	0.18	0.27
Depth—Year 2 (x_4)	0.45	0.09	0.18	0.27
Expertise—Year 2 (x_5)	0.45	0.09	0.09	0.36
Tie strength—Year 2 (x_6)	0.27	0.27	0.27	0.18
High-quality instruction—Year 2 (x_7)	0.45	0.09	0.27	0.18

(Note that in some of the rows the probabilities may appear not to add up to 1 due to rounding.)

calculate $H(Y)$. We will use the *abcd* values from the first row, the *Depth—Year 1* variable. The calculation for the outcome uncertainty is as follows:

$$H(Y) = -p(y = 1) \log_2 (p(y = 1)) - p(y = 0) \log_2 (p(y = 0))$$
$$= -(a + b) \log_2 (a + b) - (c + d) \log_2 (c + d)$$
$$= -(0.18 + 0.36) \log_2 (0.18 + 0.36)$$
$$- (0.09 + 0.36) \log_2 (0.09 + 0.36)$$
$$= -0.54 \log_2 (0.54) + 0.45 \log_2 (0.45)$$
$$= -0.54 (-0.89) + 0.45 -1.15)$$
$$= 0.99$$

In the forest loss example, the outcome uncertainty, $H(Y)$, was 0.81. In this example, it is 0.99, which means that in the absence of information from any of the independent variables, there is nearly perfect uncertainty about the outcome. Without any other information, we can't do much better than a coin flip in predicting third-year teaching success.

How much better can we do if we have the information about the other values collected for this study? The answer to that question comes from the conditional value of H for each of our independent variables. Here are the *abcd* calculations for the effect of network expertise in Year 2 on our uncertainty about the outcome Y:

$$H(Y|X) = - [d (\log_2 (d) - \log_2 (b + d)) + b (\log_2 (b) - \log_2 (b + d))]$$
$$- [c (\log_2 (c) - \log_2 (a + c)) + a (\log_2 (a) - \log_2 (a + c))]$$
$$= - [0.36 (\log_2 (0.36) - \log_2 (0.09 + 0.36))$$
$$+ (0.09 (\log_2 (0.09) - \log_2 (0.09 + 0.36))]$$
$$- [0.09 (\log_2 (0.09) - \log_2 (0.46 + 0.09))$$
$$+ (0.46 (\log_2 (0.46) - \log_2 (0.46 + 0.09))]$$
$$= - [0.36 ((-1.46) - (-1.14)) + 0.09 ((-3.46) - (-1.14))]$$
$$- [0.09 ((-3.46) - (-0.86)) + 0.46 ((-1.14) - (-0.86))]$$
$$= - ((-0.12) + (-0.21)) - ((-0.23) + (-0.13))$$
$$= 0.69$$

Our uncertainty about the *Quality of instruction in the third year* (Y) is reduced significantly from almost complete uncertainty (0.99) to uncertainty of 0.69 if we have knowledge about the value of *Network expertise in Year 2*. The change from 0.99 to 0.69 is an uncertainty reduction of 0.30 or about one third.

The information metrics for the teacher network data are shown in Table 5.13. We also include here the direction of the relationships, all of which are positive with the interesting exception of tie strength in the second year, which is negatively related to the high-quality instruction outcome but provides very little information value. Again, this is calculated from the joint probabilities from Table 5.12. If the sum of the joint probabilities when X and Y are jointly 1 or 0 is greater than the sum of the joint probabilities when X and Y take on different values, then the relationship is positive.

Compare: What Does It All Mean?

The information metrics in Table 5.13 show us that teacher network expertise in the second year (x_5) provides the most information about the likelihood of high-quality instruction in the third year (Y). We can also see that we gain almost nothing from most of the other variables. Only network depth in the second year (x_4) provides any other appreciable information about the likelihood of high-quality instruction in the third year (Y). These findings may

Table 5.13 Conditional Information Entropy and Mutual Information (Uncertainty Reduction)

High-Quality Instruction Conditions	Conditional Information Entropy $H(Y\|X)$	Mutual Information $I(Y; X) = H(Y) - H(Y\|X)$	Direction
Depth—Year 1 (x_1)	0.98	0.02	Positive
Expertise—Year 1 (x_2)	0.99	0.00	Positive
Tie strength—Year 1 (x_3)	0.94	0.05	Negative
Depth—Year 2 (x_4)	0.84	0.15	Positive
Expertise—Year 2 (x_5)	0.69	0.30	Positive
Tie strength—Year 2 (x_6)	0.99	0.01	Positive
High-quality instruction—Year 2 (x_7)	0.94	0.05	Positive

The first column in this table shows the absolute amount of uncertainty we will have about the success of high-quality instruction in the third year given that we know the value of each of the independent variables. Lower values show less uncertainty. The second column (mutual information) shows the reduction in uncertainty for the success of high-quality instruction in the third year given knowledge of each of the independent variables.

have significant implications for decisions about potential policies and resource allocations designed to improve the quality of instruction.

Example 3—Medicine: Effective Nursing Care

Our third example comes from the field of medicine or, more specifically, from nursing. Frank Donnelly and Richard Wiechula (2013) published a short article in the journal *Nurse Researcher* that was aimed substantively at discussing factors that contributed to more successful clinical experiences in the education of nurses. At the same time, their primary goal was to demonstrate the benefits of QCA as a methodology for nursing research. Our goal is to take this one step further to show how information theory could further illuminate the results of their study. (We will return to integrating information theory and QCA in Chapter 7.)

Quantify: Setting Up a Truth Table

The Donnelly and Wiechula (2013) study examines 16 nursing students. The outcome of interest is a dichotomous measure for effective nursing interventions over an 8-hour nursing shift (*OUTC*). Five independent variables were reported in the study. Duration (*DURA*) is the minimum number of clinical placement hours required in the students' educational program. Preparation (*PREP*) was a measure of the students' sense of the effectiveness of their preparation for nursing work. Benefit (*BENF*) measured the students' sense of the educational effectiveness of their clinical placement. Lectures (*NSPL*) tried to capture their recall of relevant university lectures. Experiences (*NSPO*) recorded whether the students had had clinical opportunities to care for patients with "nurse-sensitive patient outcomes." All of these variables were coded in a binary {0, 1} format by the original authors. Table 5.14 presents the raw data in a truth table.

The dependent outcome variable is the effectiveness of nursing interventions. We want to know how much we can learn about this outcome from knowing the values of the

Table 5.14 Truth Table for Donnelly and Wiechula (2013) Data on Clinical Training for Nurses

	x_1: DURA	x_2: PREP	x_3: BENF	x_4: NSPL	x_5: NSPO	Y: OUTC
Case 1	0	1	0	0	1	0
Case 2	0	0	1	0	1	0
Case 4	1	1	1	1	1	0
Case 5	0	0	1	0	1	0
Case 7	0	1	1	0	1	1
Case 8	0	1	1	0	1	1
Case 10	1	1	1	0	1	1
Case 11	1	1	1	1	1	0
Case 12	1	1	1	1	1	0
Case 13	0	1	1	0	1	1
Case 14	1	1	1	0	1	1
Case 16	0	1	1	0	0	0
Case 17	0	1	1	1	0	0
Case 18	0	0	1	0	0	0
Case 19	0	0	1	0	1	0
Case 20	0	0	1	0	0	0

Data from Donnelly and Wiechula (2013, p. 9). Case numbering is from the published study.

independent variables. The necessary data have already been collected and quantified into simple binary values. We are ready to turn to the counting part of the process.

Count: Calculating the Probabilities

The 16 cases in the nursing study have a split of 5 successful outcomes and 11 unsuccessful outcomes. Adding the information about the co-occurrences of the independent variables, we can count up the number of times the different possible combinations of values for each independent variable and the outcome variable. With five independent variables and our four possible combinations, this will give us a table with 20 cells. These simple counts are shown in Table 5.15.

Adding up our data about the overall number of successful and unsuccessful outcomes, as shown in Table 5.16, will set us up to do our joint probability calculations.

Table 5.15   Counting the X and Y Combinations

Effective Nursing Intervention Conditions	Data Counts: (x, y)			
	Count $(x_i = 1, y = 1)$	Count $(x_i = 0, y = 1)$	Count $(x_i = 1, y = 0)$	Count $(x_i = 0, y = 0)$
DURA (x_1)	2	3	3	8
PREP (x_2)	5	0	6	5
BENF (x_3)	5	0	10	1
NSPL (x_4)	0	5	4	7
NSPO (x_5)	5	0	7	4

Table 5.16   Other Quantities to Count

Total number of cases n	16
Total number of Success outcomes $(Y = 1)$	5
Total number of Other outcomes $(Y = 0)$	11

To calculate the joint probabilities, we divide the counts in each cell of Table 5.15 by the total number of cases (16). As in the tropical forest example, some of our joint

Table 5.17 Joint Probabilities

Effective Nursing Intervention Conditions	Joint Probability: $p(x, y) = \text{count}(x, y)/n$			
	$p(x_i = 1, y = 1)$	$p(x_i = 0, y = 1)$	$p(x_i = 1, y = 0)$	$p(x_i = 0, y = 0)$
	a	b	c	d
DURA (x_1)	0.13	0.19	0.19	0.50
PREP (x_2)	0.31	0.00*	0.38	0.31
BENF (x_3)	0.31	0.00*	0.63	0.06
NSPL (x_4)	0.00*	0.31	0.25	0.44
NSPO (x_5)	0.31	0.00	0.44	0.25

Note that the zero values (with asterisk) have been adjusted by adding 0.00001 (in some of the rows the probabilities may appear not to add up to 1 due to rounding).

probabilities are zero (indicated in Table 5.17 with asterisks). To ensure that the log is defined for these cases, we will again approximate the joint probability off zero by 0.00001. This small adjustment does not show up in the table due to rounding but is important to facilitate the later calculations. The results are displayed in Table 5.17.

Compute: Calculating the Information Metrics

We begin, again, with calculating the total outcome uncertainty $H(Y)$. For the *abcd* method, we can calculate this from any of the x rows. We will again use the first variable (*DURA*):

$$H(Y) = -p(y = 1) \log_2 (p(y = 1)) - p(y = 0) \log_2 (p(y = 0))$$
$$= -(a + b) \log_2 (a + b) - (c + d) \log_2 (c + d)$$
$$= -(0.13 + .19) \log_2 (0.13 + .19)$$
$$\quad - (0.19 + 0.50) \log_2 (0.19 + 0.50)$$
$$= -(0.31 \log_2 (0.31)) - (0.69 \log_2 (0.69))$$
$$= -(-0.53) - (-0.37)$$
$$= 0.90$$

If there is any useful information at all in the five explanatory factors, we should be able to reduce this very high uncertainty.

The conditional values, $H(Y|X)$, and the mutual information values, $I(Y; X)$, for each independent variable can be easily computed from the joint probabilities (the *abcd* values) we calculated in Table 5.17. The mutual information score again shows how much each factor reduces the uncertainty of the outcome variable. The conditional information entropy and mutual information values are displayed in Table 5.18.

Compare: What Does It All Mean?

Table 5.18 shows us how much we reduce the uncertainty about effective nursing intervention outcomes by knowing about each of our independent variables. The clear takeaway here is that none of the variables really has a particularly appreciable information relationship with improving nurse-sensitive patient outcomes. Asking students about the sense of preparation would be modestly helpful, but that still only reduces our uncertainty from 0.90 to 0.69. Operationalizing and measuring a sense of preparation validly and reliably could also be very challenging, as this notion could be ambiguous or evolving.

Table 5.18 Conditional Information Entropy and Mutual Information (Uncertainty Reduction)

Effective Nursing Intervention Conditions	Conditional Information Entropy $H(Y|X)$	Mutual Information $I(Y; X) = H(Y) - H(Y|X)$	Direction
DURA (x_1)	0.89	0.01	Positive
PREP (x_2)	0.69	0.21	Positive
BENF (x_3)	0.86	0.04	Positive
NSPL (x_4)	0.74	0.16	Negative
NSPO (x_5)	0.74	0.16	Positive

The first column in this table shows the absolute amount of uncertainty we will have about the success of high-quality instruction in the third year given that we know the value of each of the independent variables. Lower values show less uncertainty. The second column (mutual information) shows the reduction in uncertainty for the success of high-quality instruction in the third year given knowledge of each of the independent variables. The greatest information gain (reduction in uncertainty) comes from knowing the value of PREP (the students' sense of preparation for nursing work).

As is often the case, the failure of some variables to convey information about an outcome is, in itself, of potential interest. In this example, more hours of clinical placement (*DURA*) in nursing school did not have an appreciable impact on the uncertainty about nursing care outcomes. And a student's sense of the value of that clinical placement (*BENF*) is similarly nonconsequential. On the other hand, a new nurse's ability to recall a lecture on "nurse-sensitive patient outcomes" was an indicator that good outcomes were actually less likely.

This study was aimed toward demonstrating the benefits of QCA, a subject to which we will turn in Chapter 7. Even so, it is worth noting that the original study did not provide any direct analysis of the individual impact of these variables, beyond the opportunity for visual assessment of the truth table. The information metrics, then, can significantly enhance our ability to systematically understand and analyze this kind of data, with potentially lifesaving implications in medical fields, among others.

Conclusion

In each of these three cases, the application of information metrics allowed us to gain a better sense of the relative effects of the selected factors on the outcomes of interest. In their original published forms, each of these studies relied on subjective assessment to disentangle the magnitude of effects.

These results can strengthen the ability of scholars to understand and communicate the results of their case studies. In the same manner, practitioners and policy makers should find it easier to identify critical variables that might provide more effective outcomes or policy levers.

Our next step is to look at how we can use information metrics to understand the sensitivity of our results to the inclusion or exclusion of specific cases.

Additional resources are provided at http://study.sagepub.com/drozdova.

Sensitivity Analysis— Entropy, Inference, and Error

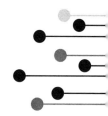

Among the contributions of Claude Shannon's unifying theory of communication was to show that information could be transmitted and decoded accurately, essentially without error. Prior to Shannon, it had been taken for granted that the more information you were sending or the faster you were trying to send it, the greater the probability of error. Shannon's metric allowed for calculating the channel capacity that would be required for the transmission of any given information with "all but an arbitrarily small fraction of the errors" (Shannon, 1948, p. 20). Shannon's insight paved the way for the digital revolution that allows huge amounts of information to zip around without consequential error. The concepts of information and error have, therefore, been intimately linked from the beginning of the Information Age. In this chapter, we turn to the problem of understanding and handling error in the use of information theory for comparative case study analysis.

Here we need to return to a little of the research philosophy we presented in Chapter 1 (Figure 1.1). We can look at all case study work in three phases. The first two phases involve the theoretical conceptualization and design of the case study, the selection of cases, and the actual collection and coding of data (Yin, 2014). These steps are universal to all case studies and are not significantly changed by the use of information metrics, except to the degree that our approach requires setting up of a set of structured-focused comparisons and recording the data as binary {0, 1} measures. The real focus of our approach is the third phase: the systematic analysis of the case study results.

The analytic phase of the case study analysis can be further broken down into three steps. The first of these is to consolidate the case results into a single truth table. The second analytic step is to clearly identify the relationships between the independent variables and the dependent variable in the collected data. This is the primary leverage of the systematic information approach. The information metric provides an exact measure of the amount of information about the variation in the dependent variable that is contained in an independent variable for a given set of measures from a given set of cases.

The final step in the analytic process is to draw inferences from the results of the case study to the real world. This is a core challenge of both large-N and small-n studies but is clearly more acute for small-n work. How can we be confident that our research findings apply in the world?

A gap always exists between the selection of cases we have chosen to analyze and the larger world. In large-N statistics, we gain inferential leverage from the possibility that the data set is a reasonably random representative selection from the population. If the data are adequately random, the central limit theorem and other foundational concepts of statistical analysis can help us understand how to infer from a random sample to the population. As we argued in Chapter 1, these standard statistical procedures are often unreliable or inapplicable in small-n analysis.

The ability to draw valid inferences from the selected case studies still depends on analytic or contingent generalizations and assessments about the character of case selection. Information theory provides a concrete set of measures with relative magnitudes to systematically guide assessment. The information metric is a rigorous and reproducible basis for understanding the relationship between independent and dependent variables within the selected set of cases. The information metric offers a significant improvement over traditional case study methodologies, but it isn't a magic wand that can overcome all of the limitations of small-n analytics.

Traditional small-n case analysis often depends on one's qualitative assessment of the connection between the cases and the larger population. Ideally, this assessment should be driven by theory and verified by evidence, but in the absence of systematic tools for evaluating case results, there is a risk of simply making a subjective judgment call. If scholars believe that their cases are representative, they would expect the same information conditions to hold in the world at large. But, there may be many sources of uncertainty in complex broader real-world problems. We may also believe that our cases are especially informative. They may be "most-likely" or "least-likely" cases (Eckstein, 1975; George & Bennett, 2005, p. 121). They may be selected for theoretical purposes in other ways that increase our confidence that they can help us learn about the more general phenomena.

The inferential leverage that comes from the ability to observe the context of the data and the relationships within them is one of the advantages of working with small-n analysis. This approach falls within "contingent generalization" (George & Smoke, 1974). George and Bennett (2005) put contingent generalization at the center of case-based techniques. Other scholars have advanced similar arguments for the benefits of case study methods. Ragin (1987, p. 31) uses the term *modest generalizations* to characterize the inferential leverage of case study research, and Yin (2014) uses the term *analytic generalizations*.

Improving the first phase of the analysis step, making the analysis of the cases themselves more systematic and rigorous, does not solve all small-n challenges, but it can provide a firmer foundation from which to make inferences. Moreover, these information techniques give us new tools for assessing the impact of the individual cases and coding on our results. In this way, we can better understand the sensitivity of the findings to inclusion or exclusion of specific cases or to errors in data collection or coding. Understanding the sensitivities can also give us important insights into the data and into the character and quality of our inferences.

Confidence Intervals and the Information Metric

Anyone coming from a large-N background will be familiar with the notion of confidence intervals, or credible intervals if you are of the Bayesian persuasion. In large-N statistical work, we take a sufficiently large random sample from a population and then calculate a range around a point prediction in which we have high statistical confidence that the true quantities of interest will be found, based on the observed values in the sample. In other words, we can find a probability that the estimated interval contains the unknown parameter of interest. This approach is a strong tool for gaining leverage on the inference problem in large-N research.

There are several ways to calculate confidence intervals for the entropy measure (Esteban & Morales, 1995; Roulston, 1999; Sveshnikov, 1978, p. 288). We are not going to recommend them here. There are four reasons we think these statistical tools are not appropriate for the kinds of case studies we are addressing in this book.

In the first place, our goal is to provide a straightforward approach to case study analysis that is manageable for students and practitioners with widely varying quantitative backgrounds, including scholars who may not be interested in delving into more in-depth statistics. The conceptual workarounds and calculations required for estimating confidence intervals for a small number of cases involve significantly more complex calculations. Thus, approaches to confidence intervals for information measures are beyond the scope appropriate for the introductory level and the intended audience for this book. A single mutual information number for each variable is more elegant and ultimately sufficient for comparative case analysis. This is a simple informative tool to add to a primarily qualitative analysis toolkit for case study research.

Second, these techniques are often designed for the much more challenging process of estimating entropy scores for research problems involving variables that can take on many different or even continuous values, and thus where mutual information scores cannot be directly calculated but must be estimated even in the sample space (Paninski, 2003). In our application for comparative case studies, information metrics do not make point predictions for which confidence intervals are typically designed. Rather, mutual information provides a direct measure, based on the analyzed cases, of the relative information content of the different independent variables about case outcomes of interest. Confidence intervals could provide relative ranges but only at a high computational cost and with dubious additional leverage. In our approach, limiting the analysis to binary coding of both the independent and dependent variables gives us a complete picture of the conditional probabilities and the ability to calculate entropy and mutual information directly and precisely, with straightforward leverage for interpreting the comparative case results.

Third, the construction of confidence intervals requires an assumption that the cases are a random selection from some larger population. This, as we discuss in Chapter 3, is not often the case for small-n studies, where the cases are typically selected for particular theoretical purposes, not for statistical significance. The quality of the confidence intervals will itself depend on our confidence that the cases were selected at random.

Finally, small-n case studies remain small n—part of a methodology designed explicitly for in-depth qualitative research and particular types of contingent and analytic generalizations that are conceptually distinct from and complementary to traditional statistical techniques. By design, typically there will not be that many cases, which means that even if we are satisfied that the cases are a random selection, the confidence intervals are still likely to be relatively wide. Their primary function will then be to verify that the mutual information number falls inside the confidence interval calculated at a reasonable confidence level (e.g., 99%, 95%, or 90% at least) to establish statistical significance of the results. While helpful as an additional verification by a different method that adds confidence to our overall knowledge, it is not statistical significance that such case studies typically seek.

The benefit of applying information theory to comparative case study is that it helps us precisely understand the information content of the cases we have. It cannot magically overcome all of the challenges of drawing inferences from a very small data set.

How, then, are we to think about inferences with the use of information theory to make small-n analysis more systematic?

A real-world example can help demonstrate the procedures for assessing case study results in terms of these sensitivities. This example is about environmental policy.

Analytic Leverage for a Study of Environmental Incentives

The reduction of municipal garbage production has become an important environmental goal for a number of reasons, including the limited availability of suitable landfill space and the impact of toxins in waste disposal strategies. In the early 1990s, a group of researchers at Duke University undertook a study of residential garbage on behalf of the Environmental Protection Agency (EPA) to look at the effects of unit pricing disposal fees on the per capita quantity of municipal solid waste (Miranda & Aldy, 1996). The study authors developed a very careful structured-focused comparison asking a consistent set of research questions to assess 14 explanatory variables across nine communities. Although the authors provide a summary table for each individual variable and a more detailed descriptive summary for each case, they provide no systematic table to summarize the study as a whole and to provide a direct way to visualize or assess the overarching relationships between the independent and dependent variables.

To that end, and for our purposes here, we have translated their results into a set of binary {0, 1} measures of 11 independent variables and 2 dependent variables (3 of the independent variables that had perfectly overlapping values were consolidated—*California, High housing costs,* and *High garbage fees*). The first dependent variable, shown in Table 6.1, is simply whether or not the amount of residential solid waste was reduced after the introduction of unit pricing

Table 6.1 Truth Table for Unit Pricing and Waste Reduction Data

	California (High Housing Costs and Garbage Fees)	Unit Pricing Pre-1990	Large Cities (Pop > 100,000)	Urban Communities	Median Household Income > $35k	Waste Collection Primarily Private	Mandatory Rather Than Opt-In Recycling	Recycling Fee	Use of TV/Radio to Publicize	Tipping Fee > $30/ton	Fee per Gallon/Week < $0.05	Total Waste Volume Reduced
Downers Grove	0	0	0	0	1	1	1	0	1	1	0	1
Glendale	1	0	1	0	0	0	0	0	0	0	1	1
Grand Rapids	0	1	1	1	0	1	0	1	1	1	1	0
Hoffman Estates	0	0	0	0	1	1	1	0	0	1	0	1
Lansing	0	1	1	1	0	0	1	1	1	1	0	0
Pasadena	1	0	1	0	1	0	1	0	0	0	1	0
San Jose	1	0	1	1	1	1	1	0	1	0	0	0
Santa Monica	1	0	0	0	1	0	1	0	1	1	0	1
Woodstock	0	1	0	0	0	1	1	0	0	1	0	1

The binary values shown here were coded by the current authors. California was substituted for the study variables for high garbage fees and housing values, as high garbage fees (over $2.00 per month) and high housing prices (median house value over $150,000) were both perfectly coterminous with the division between the four California cities and the five midwestern cities. More detail on these data and our revisions can be found at http://study.sagepub.com/drozdova.

(i.e., paying fees according to the amount of waste generated). The second dependent variable, to which we will return a little later, is based on the reduction in solid waste sent to a landfill or incinerators. Table 6.2 summarizes the results of the study with the first dependent variable.

The total uncertainty in these data is very high. There is a near-even split in the outcomes with five cases of successful waste reduction and four unsuccessful cases. Total uncertainty (H) is 0.99, which means that without the information from our independent variables, we have nearly perfect uncertainty about which communities were going to successfully reduce their waste volume.

Table 6.2 shows the information structure for these 11 independent variables, sorted from the most to the least informative. Having a large population or being an urban city are the most informative factors for predicting whether unit pricing will reduce solid waste, although both are negatively related to this outcome. Smaller populations and nonurban municipalities are the most likely to have reduced their solid wastes. These two factors have significant overlap, an issue we will turn to in Chapter 7. A recycling fee is one of the few variables over which policy makers have control that is informative about the outcome. As would be expected, the relationship is negative, so having a recycling fee means less diversion of recyclables from the solid waste stream. But, this finding probably merits more investigation since there are only two communities with recycling fees (Lansing and Grand Rapids), and they implement it in quite different ways. These important implications are overlooked in the report for the EPA

Table 6.2 Entropy Metrics for Waste Reduction Data

	Conditional Entropy	Mutual Information	Direction
Large cities	**0.40**	**0.59**	Negative
Urban communities	0.43	0.56	Negative
Recycling fee	0.67	0.32	Negative
Use of TV/radio to publicize	0.90	0.09	Negative
Unit pricing pre-1990	0.92	0.07	Negative
Tipping fee > $30/ton	0.92	0.07	Positive
Fee per gallon/week < $0.05	0.92	0.07	Negative
California	0.98	0.01	Negative
Median household income > $35k	0.98	0.01	Positive
Waste collection primarily private	0.98	0.01	Positive
Mandatory rather than opt-in recycling	0.99	0.00	Positive

but point to potentially important areas for further investigations and policy tools for effecting change. The other variables are essentially noninformative. There is very little reduction in uncertainty about the outcome that comes from knowing their values.

Already we have gained some analytic leverage for these cases. Neither of these insights about the challenges of encouraging waste reduction in large and urban cities was addressed in the original report. We can go further with this example, however, by also looking at the effects of the different cases on the mutual information scores.

The Information Metric and the Problem of Inference

The reason for analyzing a set of cases is almost always to draw inferences about the world at large and often about informing policy or practical decisions. We select a set of cases that we believe can tell us something about the larger world, especially when—following the principles set out in Chapter 3—they are systematically drawn and scientifically analyzed within a theoretic framework. In the solid waste unit pricing study, it is clear that the EPA was looking for an actionable understanding of the interventions or other best practices that might improve waste management outcomes in other cities across the United States. These nine communities were studied in the hopes of generating inferences about things that could be done in other communities.

Our argument is that even just applying the information metric to a set of cases is already a significant enhancement for the subjective analysis that has heretofore been the primary approach to assessing case study results. As we saw earlier, information analysis gave us new insights about the data collected for understanding the factors that might contribute to municipal solid waste reduction. Beyond that, however, the information approach gives us additional tools, of only slightly increased complexity, that can help us assess some of the sources and the extent of potential inferential error.

Sensitivity Analysis

The very fact that one is using comparative case studies is a strong indicator that the domain of interest has the potential for analytical error. If we were working with a mechanically deterministic system, there would be no need for comparative cases. One would just trace through the mechanism and then perfectly characterize the chain of causes and effects. Instead, we use small-*n* or large-*N* studies to help us understand the broader world through a closer study of some smaller part of it. This introduces the possibility of inferential error.

All small-n studies have to cross this inferential gap. For this, they will require some degree of subjective assessment. Information metrics cannot eliminate this gap. But to the degree that they provide a more structured understanding of the data we have, they can discipline the subjective move across the inference gap and strengthen it with some objective indicators of the information content of the results drawn from that data based on the analyzed cases and factors. Beyond the basic information metrics, we can get a better sense of our data and results by looking at how sensitive the information metrics are to possible variation.

Sensitivity analysis can improve our understanding of the information contours in the cases we do have. It can provide additional insights and fundamentally strengthen a well-designed case study. The most straightforward and intuitive way to do this is to look at the effects of each of the individual cases on the entropy and mutual information measures.

Dropped-Case Analysis

Our first approach is to look at the effect of removing each individual case from the information analysis. How sensitive is the mutual information score to the inclusion or exclusion of any particular case? Cases that have a particularly large effect are worth exploring more closely. They may be anomalies for which it could be fruitful to look more carefully to try to identify what makes them different. It could also be, however, that outliers are mistakes. If a case does not fit with the other data, it is more likely that it was mismeasured or miscoded. Of course, it is important not to make post hoc judgments to reject inconvenient data. Indeed, these may be the most critical cases that warrant the most analytic care. At a minimum, creating a truth table can make the data patterns explicit to help identify such mismatched cases.

To assess the sensitivity of the results to the particular cases, we simply rerun the analysis repeatedly, leaving one case out each time. While this analysis is conceptually straightforward, to do it efficiently probably requires the use of more sophisticated computational tools. You could do it with Excel by simply duplicating your worksheet several times and dropping a different case each time. This could be a little tedious but with very few cases is probably manageable.

Alternatively, this is a relatively easy task for a scripted computer language such as R, which is rapidly becoming the dominant computer language for statistical analysis. R has a steep learning curve, but it can be effectively used by beginners (Gaubatz, 2014). In Appendix B and on the website that accompanies this book (http://study.sagepub.com/drozdova), we have provided the R code for doing all of the analyses in this book, including automating dropped-case analysis.

Figure 6.1 is a straightforward dot chart (Cleveland, 1993) showing the individual effects of dropping each case on the mutual information score for several of the independent variables. This exercise provides a number of potentially important insights. We see here,

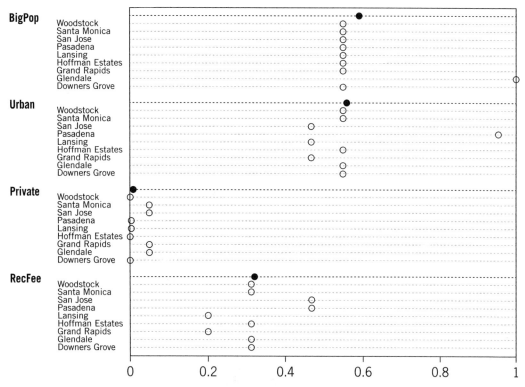

BigPop
Woodstock
Santa Monica
San Jose
Pasadena
Lansing
Hoffman Estates
Grand Rapids
Glendale
Downers Grove

Urban
Woodstock
Santa Monica
San Jose
Pasadena
Lansing
Hoffman Estates
Grand Rapids
Glendale
Downers Grove

Private
Woodstock
Santa Monica
San Jose
Pasadena
Lansing
Hoffman Estates
Grand Rapids
Glendale
Downers Grove

RecFee
Woodstock
Santa Monica
San Jose
Pasadena
Lansing
Hoffman Estates
Grand Rapids
Glendale
Downers Grove

0   0.2   0.4   0.6   0.8   1

This figure shows the effect on the entropy measure of dropping each case for a selected set of variables. The solid dots represent the mutual information score when all cases are included. The open dots show the mutual information score when each corresponding case on the y-axis is dropped from the analysis. Variable names have been abbreviated and include Large cities (BigPop), Urban communities (Urban), Waste collection primarily private (Private), and Recycling fee (RecFee).

Figure 6.1   Dropped-Case Analysis

for example, that the mutual information score for the variable indicating that garbage service is private is very stable. Its very low contribution to uncertainty reduction is relatively unaffected by the exclusion of any particular case. On the other hand, we can see from the top panel of Figure 6.1 that Glendale is a critical outlier for the *Big population* variable. Glendale is the only large city with a successful outcome. Without Glendale, population size would be perfectly informative of successful solid waste reduction programs. All the small cities in this study succeeded in reducing their waste output. None of the large cities, except for Glendale, pulled this off. This policy-relevant implication is overlooked in the report for the EPA but points to a potentially fruitful area for further investigation. How Glendale succeeded where all other large municipalities failed is an important puzzle in these data.

Similarly, we can see that Pasadena has an outsized effect on the *Urban* variable. No urban area succeeded in reducing its solid waste production. All the nonurban municipalities had reductions with the singular exception of Pasadena. A more careful examination of what might have gone wrong in Pasadena could be very important.

The other variables exhibit less variation in the dropped-case analysis. Even so, we can see in Figure 6.2 that Glendale again stands out for its low tipping costs (the disposal fees imposed by landfills) but relatively high fees for waste producers. The implications of that combination may be another area ripe for further analysis.

We can summarize the effects of the dropped-case analysis in terms of either the cases or the variables. Table 6.3 shows the mean and the maximum change in the mutual information score for each variable. We can see here that the mean variation in the information scores is relatively small for all of the variables. The maximum variation is more variable. The California, high income, private, and mandatory recycling information scores change very

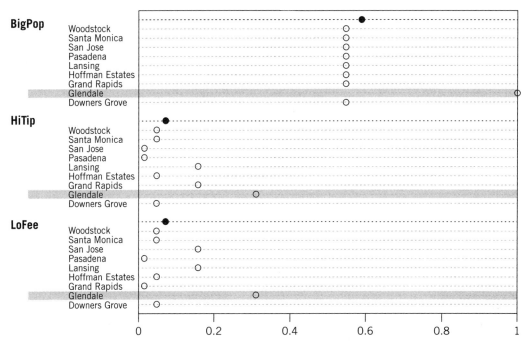

This figure highlights the effect of dropping each city on the mutual information scores for the three variables where the city of Glendale has a particularly large effect. If Glendale had not been included in the study, the information effects of high tipping costs (HiTip) and low garbage fees (LoFee) would be much higher. Without Glendale in the study, the variable for being a large city (BigPop) would be perfectly informative about the success of solid waste reduction programs.

Figure 6.2 Garbage in Glendale

Table 6.3 Mean and Maximum Variation in Mutual Information Scores From Dropping Individual Cases

Variable	Mean Variation	Maximum Variation
California	0.02	0.04
Unit pricing pre-1990	0.07	0.24
Large cities	0.08	0.41
Urban communities	0.08	0.40
Median household income > $35k	0.02	0.04
Waste collection primarily private	0.02	0.04
Mandatory rather than opt-in recycling	0.03	0.14
Recycling fee	0.06	0.15
Use of TV/radio to publicize	0.08	0.26
Tipping fee > $30/ton	0.07	0.24
Tipping fee per gallon/week < $0.05	0.07	0.24

This table shows the mean and maximum change by variable in the mutual information score when each case is dropped.

little with the inclusion or exclusion of any one case. Each of the rest of the variables has about the same amount of mean change, between 0.06 and 0.08. They are all relatively stable, with the exceptions of the large effects we see in Figure 6.1 from Glendale and Pasadena for the *Large cities* and *Urban communities* variables, respectively.

Table 6.4 shows the mean change in the mutual information score for each case. That is, it shows the mean effect of dropping one case across all of the variables. Here we see that Glendale and Pasadena are the most unusual. Their inclusion in this study has significant effects on the information metrics for several of the independent variables. Again, a closer look into these two cases might be particularly appropriate for clarifying the results and enhancing comparative rigor. Such clarity will be especially important if policy conclusions are to be drawn from the studies.

Dropped-case analysis allows us to see the impact of each case on our analytic conclusions. Importantly, these are insights that do not depend on randomized case selection. Ultimately, whether a given case warrants additional attention has to be a substantive question rather than a simple response to the dropped-case analysis, but understanding the impact of each case can be an important starting point for thinking through that issue.

At the end of the day, it remains critical to remember the principles of case selection outlined in Chapter 3. It is interesting and valuable in terms of potential policy implications to see the effects of each case, and this analysis can, again, help guide a more nuanced and subjective assessment of the cases. It is essential not to simply engage in post hoc case selection. The move from specifying the

Table 6.4   Mean and Maximum Change in All Variables for Each Dropped Case

City	Mean Change in Mutual Information Without City	Maximum Change in Mutual Information Without City
Downers Grove	0.02	0.10
Glendale	0.11	0.41
Grand Rapids	0.06	0.12
Hoffman Estates	0.02	0.04
Lansing	0.05	0.12
Pasadena	0.10	0.40
San Jose	0.06	0.15
Santa Monica	0.03	0.10
Woodstock	0.04	0.24

This table shows the mean and maximum effect of dropping each case on the information scores across all of the variables.

relationships between variables in the set of analyzed cases to inferring that those same relationships hold in the general population requires confidence that the cases are appropriately selected.

Outcome Coding Sensitivity

The dropped-case analysis focuses on the effects of each case on the mutual information scores for the relationship between the outcome and each independent variable. Another sensitivity measure would be to look at how the results change if the outcome scoring changes. This allows us to consider the critical question of whether the outcomes have been properly coded.

As discussed earlier, the environmental study offers a second dependent variable, looking at the reduction in landfill and incinerated solid waste. For the first dependent variable, the overall amount of solid waste, turning the outcome into a binary {0, 1} measure was straightforward: Cities that reduced their solid waste output were coded 1, and others (i.e., those that did not change or those that increased their solid waste output) were coded 0. The reduction in landfill/incinerator use is a little more subjective to code as binary since all of the studied cities had some level of reduction. Subject matter experts may have strong views about the appropriate cutoff threshold for identifying a successful or unsuccessful solid waste reduction outcome. We could start with two different cutoff levels: a greater than 10% reduction or a greater than 25% reduction. These two coding conventions, along with the original continuous outcome, are set out in Table 6.5.

Table 6.5   Landfill and Incinerated Waste Reduction Outcomes

City	LIR	LIR10 (10% or Greater Reduction)	LIR25 (25% or Greater Reduction)
Downers Grove	−0.24	1	0
Glendale	−0.34	1	1
Grand Rapids	−0.22	1	0
Hoffman Estates	−0.39	1	1
Lansing	−0.50	1	1
Pasadena	−0.60	0	0
San Jose	−0.22	1	0
Santa Monica	−0.70	0	0
Woodstock	−0.30	1	1

This table shows the actual reduction in landfill/incinerator solid waste with two different cutoff points for the binary coding. The first, LIR10, identifies those communities that decreased their solid waste by more than 10%. The second, LIR25, identifies those communities that achieved a greater than 25% reduction. LIR means landfill/incinerator reduction.

The 10% landfill or incinerator reduction cutoff yields an outcome variable with seven successes and just two failures. This yields a lower degree of outcome uncertainty, $H(Y) = 0.76$, because success would usually be a pretty good guess about the outcome. The 25% landfill or incinerator reduction cutoff yields an outcome variable with four successes and five failures. This is a nearly perfect degree of outcome uncertainty, $H(Y) = 0.99$. The mutual information (uncertainty reduction) metrics for these alternative outcome variables are displayed in Table 6.6 with abbreviated independent variable names.

For the 10% reduction breakpoint, being in California (which, remember, means high fees and high housing costs), having mostly private collection programs, and being a high-income city are the most informative independent variables. High income and being in California make success less likely, while private programs increase the likelihood of success.

We can see, however, that these results are quite sensitive to the choice of cutoff point for coding a successful outcome. If we increase the cutoff point to a 25% reduction, Downers Grove, Grand Rapids, and San Jose fall out of the success category. At the 25% level, there are not many strong predictors. High-income communities are again less likely to reduce their garbage output. This is intuitive, as they are less sensitive to the usage fees that are the subject of this study. More surprising is that the use of media to publicize the programs is also associated with reduced program efficacy. This variable was not very informative for the 10% reduction outcome variable or for the original outcome variable, which was coded 1 for any

Table 6.6 Information Metrics for LIR10 and LIR25

Variable	LIR10 Mutual Information	LIR10 Direction	LIR25 Mutual Information	LIR25 Direction
CA	0.32	Negative	0.09	Negative
Private	0.32	Positive	0.01	Negative
HiInc	0.23	Negative	0.23	Negative
Pre-1990	0.15	Positive	0.07	Positive
Urban	0.15	Positive	0.02	Negative
MandRec	0.09	Positive	0.00	Negative
RecFee	0.09	Negative	0.00	Positive
HiTip	0.03	Positive	0.02	Positive
LoFee	0.03	Negative	0.02	Negative
BigPop	0.00	Positive	0.00	Negative
Media	0.00	Positive	0.23	Negative

reduction in total solid waste output (Table 6.2). This set of findings clearly warrants more detailed study. If it holds up, it would be an obvious and more straightforward area for policy change than many of the other variables.

Several of the explanatory variables in Table 6.6 change direction from the 10% case to the 25% case. This is not surprising since in every instance at one or the other end, the mutual information is very close to zero, so it can easily flip above or below zero to change the sign.

Ultimately, interpreting Table 6.6 requires some degree of substantive expertise. What counts as a large or very large reduction in landfill or incinerator waste should be determined contextually with theoretically, empirically, and experientially informed expert assessment. Indeed, it could be that the explanatory factors for a very large reduction in landfill or incinerator waste are different from the explanatory factors for just a normal reduction in waste. In any case, we see from Table 6.6 that several of these results are sensitive to this coding choice. The analyst will likely want to draw on the original and more in-depth data from the case studies, which remain available to provide the advantages of the more nuanced understanding available in the small-*n* environment.

The same techniques used for the sensitivity of the information metrics to outcome coding can also be used to assess the sensitivity to the coding of the independent variables. This can be labor intensive, depending on the number and character of the independent variables.

It will be most appropriate for those factors where the criterion for making the binary coding {0, 1} is more ambiguous. Here, again, substantive expertise is required to make judgments about the appropriate cutoff points and their meaning. And, as discussed in Chapters 3 and 4, whichever meaningful cutoff points are selected, the binary coding criteria should clearly and measurably define two mutually exclusive categories so that the underlying data are precisely classified.

Conclusion

Information metrics can give us significant insights into the relationships within a set of small-n data. Considering the sensitivity of the entropy metrics to the inclusion or exclusion of particular cases, as well as the sensitivity of the metrics to particular coding decisions, can help cast further light on the data and the conclusions in a structured-focused case study.

In the EPA garbage study, the application of information metrics both made the study results more systematic and rigorous and provided additional insights that were not included in the original report. We saw that waste reduction appears to be considerably more difficult in high-income, large, urban cities. But, analyzing the sensitivity of these results to the specific cases helped us quickly identify the cases that stand out as having a large impact on the results. We saw, in particular, that the Glendale case may merit further attention as the only large-population city that was successful in reducing its solid waste output. But, Glendale is also coded as nonurban. All of the nonurban municipalities were successful in reducing waste, with the exception of Pasadena. That case, too, may require a closer look.

This example study also highlights that further insights might depend on understanding the patterns of how the different independent factors combine. Thus far, these measures have been used in a strictly bivariate sense: Entropy is a measure of uncertainty, and mutual information is a measure of the information value of each individual factor for understanding an outcome. It is likely that we would also benefit from knowing about the relationships between the independent variables. For this purpose, we can push the information metric further by combining it with the technique called qualitative case analysis (QCA). That is the subject of the next chapter.

Additional resources are provided at http://study.sagepub.com/drozdova.

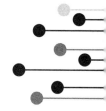

The QCA Connection

The information methods we have demonstrated are very powerful on their own and have the important advantage of being simple and straightforward to conceptualize, to calculate, and to communicate. They can, however, also be integrated with other methods to gain further leverage. In particular, as discussed at the end of Chapter 6, it would be helpful to have an approach for understanding the structure of relationships among the independent variables, the causal factors, in addition to the enhanced measures of how informative each independent variable is about the dependent variable. In this chapter, we focus on qualitative case analysis (QCA), a popular and powerful approach to understanding and visualizing the patterns of co-occurrence among variables in a small-*n* study (Ragin, 1987).

This chapter sets out the complementary relationship between using information theory for case analysis and the use of QCA, as pioneered by Charles Ragin. QCA uses Boolean logic to consolidate diverse factors into clusters of conditions. We show how information theory can strengthen QCA analysis by providing a systematic metric to assess the relative impact of the different consolidated conditions identified by QCA.

QCA is a powerful approach for identifying and thinking through the complex patterns of relationships between a set of causes and outcomes. It incorporates the classic methods of correspondence (Mill's method of agreement and difference) and counterfactual analysis. QCA focuses on the concepts of necessary and sufficient conditions. It builds on set theory and uses Boolean algebra to identify the constellations of causal conditions that connect to outcome variables. It helps to both identify and reduce causal complexity in small-*n* data.

We will focus here on what is called crisp-set QCA, which is particularly complementary to information metrics. Like information theory, it starts with truth tables, with the data organized as a set of causal factors and a single dependent variable, all coded with binary values {0, 1}.

QCA can improve information metrics by identifying patterns within the independent variables that allow for reducing the number of analytic concepts. Information metrics can improve QCA by providing a systematic tool for assessing the analytic leverage provided by each of the resulting analytic concepts in comparison to one another as well as to the original variables.

Understanding Qualitative Case Analysis (QCA)

This is not the place for a complete tutorial on QCA analysis (we have provided a list of a few introductory QCA resources at the end of this chapter). Nonetheless, given our argument that the two techniques are complementary, it is worth spending a little time on a brief overview of the QCA process. Again, we focus here on crisp-set QCA (csQCA) because it starts with the same clear truth table setup as our approach to information analysis.

QCA analysis can be done by hand (virtuous, but laborious), with stand-alone software (fs/QCA), or with add-on packages for major statistical packages (QCA or QCA3 for R or fuzzy for Stata). Sources and resources for these programs are available at the end of this chapter.

The essential and appealing logic of QCA is to look at the explanatory variables and determine which ones work together (either in their presence or absence) to produce an outcome of interest. QCA uses Boolean logic to map out the patterns, or constellations, of independent variables that are, to return to our information-theoretic terminology, informative about the outcome variable. Groups of variables are identified as "prime implicants," which can combine into "recipes" to characterize the patterns of relationships in the independent and dependent variables. QCA accepts that causality can be complex, and thus, these recipes can contain alternative groups that lead to the same outcome.

QCA builds on many of the same probability concepts we introduced in Chapter 2. "Consistency," in the QCA parlance, means that whenever X is true, it is unlikely that Y is false. Knowing that X is true consistently tells you a lot about the value of Y. This condition would be reflected in a high value for the conditional probability of Y given X. In set-theoretic terms, this means that the cases in which X is true are a subset (or nearly a subset) of the cases where Y is true. If this conditional probability is high, it means that whenever X happens, Y is highly likely to happen as well. In logical terms, this means that, with high likelihood, X is sufficient for Y.

The QCA concept of "coverage" means that whenever Y is true, it is unlikely that X is false. This is coverage in the sense that the cases where Y is true are essentially a subset of the cases in which X is true. The X is true cases "cover" all of the Y cases. This means that Y usually cannot happen without X. In logical terms, with high likelihood, X is necessary for Y.

Building from the coverage and consistency relationships, QCA identifies the combinations of factors, both in terms of their presence and their absence, that are associated with the outcome. These are set out in what are called "recipes" indicating which variables are present or absent in each consolidated factor set. The sets are identified through an iterative process of simplification, identifying rows that are paired with a single outcome but that differ on just one factor. That factor is presumed to be irrelevant and is eliminated.

This process continues until the minimum set of recipes is identified that covers all of the outcome instances.

QCA and Causal Complexity

QCA is particularly focused on the possibility of complex causality. That is, there may be multiple paths, or combinations of variables, that lead to the same outcome. Any given variable may have different effects depending on the other variables with which it combines. At a very simple level, for example, we might expect that poverty combined with an environment of high social aspirations makes civil unrest more likely, while poverty combined with an environment of low social aspirations makes civil unrest less likely (Gurr, 1970). Poverty and high or low social aspirations, individually, are insufficient to cause civil unrest. Likewise, none of them alone is necessary for this outcome, since there are other pathways to civil unrest as well.

This notion of complex causality accords with philosopher John Mackie's critical contributions to our understanding of causality (Mackie, 1965). He argues that what we really mean when we argue that X causes Y is neither that X is necessary nor that X is sufficient for Y but rather that X is an insufficient but necessary part of a set of conditions that are themselves unnecessary but sufficient for the outcome. QCA helps us assess these complex relationships, while information theory can help make the output of QCA more rigorous. It gives us a measuring stick for understanding the relative effectiveness and analytic leverage of the different causal combinations.

Where QCA and Information Metrics Differ

It is important to point out here that information metrics differ from the set-theory logic of QCA inasmuch as the information metrics are conditioned by the amount of variation in X. If X does not vary (i.e., it is almost always true or almost always false) then, a priori, it cannot be very informative about Y, even if the probability of Y given X is very high. Alternatively, information metrics will detect an underlying dependency between X and Y variables if it exists, even if slight, presumed irrelevant, or overlooked by other methods. Where QCA eliminates a factor as irrelevant, information metrics will show a dependency if mutual information is nonzero (whereas a mutual information score of zero will confirm that the variables are independent).

So, too, QCA makes a much stronger distinction between positive and negative outcomes in analysis. Information metrics treat positive and negative outcomes as perfect complements: Being informative about when the outcome will happen is the same as being informative about when the outcome will not happen. QCA's set-theoretic approach sees predicting success as different from predicting failure. This asymmetry arises from complex causality, the multiple pathways that might lead to either success or failure. The constellation of conditions that leads to success could be different from the conditions that lead to failure. Because of the existence of alternative pathways, the absence of one of the pathways for success does not automatically portend failure. In the same way, the absence of the conditions for failure does not guarantee success.

Finally, where information theory can provide precise metrics to describe the relationship between any two variables, since QCA helpfully works on aggregating conditions, it needs a minimum number of cases to be effective. Ten is the usual number given, which makes it more appropriate for midrange projects that are too small for traditional statistics but still cross that lower threshold.

Examples of Enhancing QCA With Information Metrics

QCA and Information Metrics for Ragin Ethnic Mobilization Data

Charles Ragin is the prime architect of the QCA method. We can start our discussion with a quick example drawn from his foundational book, *The Comparative Method* (1987). Ragin provides an example looking at the political mobilization of ethnic groups. His small data set includes four causal factors: the size of the subnational group (S), the linguistic abilities of the subnational group (L), the relative wealth of the group (W), and the economic growth of the region (G). The dependent variable is whether the ethnic group is politically mobilized (E). These data are displayed in Table 7.1, with the addition of case numbers.

Table 7.1 Ethnic Political Mobilization Data

	Case	S	L	W	G	E
1	Lapps, Finland	0	0	0	0	0
2	Finns, Sweden	0	0	0	0	0
3	Lapps, Sweden	0	0	0	0	0
4	Albanians, Italy	0	0	0	0	0
5	Greeks, Italy	0	0	0	0	0
6	North Frisians, Germany	0	0	0	1	1
7	Danes, Germany	0	0	0	1	1
8	Basques, France	0	0	0	1	1
9	Ladins, Italy	0	0	1	0	0

10	Magyars, Austria	0	1	0	0	0
11	Croats, Austria	0	1	0	0	0
12	Slovenes, Austria	0	1	0	0	1
13	Greenlanders, Denmark	0	1	0	0	1
14	Aalanders, Finland	0	1	1	0	0
15	Slovenes, Italy	0	1	1	1	1
16	Valdotians, Italy	0	1	1	1	0
17	Sards, Italy	1	0	0	0	1
18	Galicians, Spain	1	0	0	0	1
19	West Frisians, Netherlands	1	0	0	1	1
20	Catalans, France	1	0	0	1	1
21	Occitans, France	1	0	0	1	1
22	Welsh, Great Britain	1	0	0	1	0
23	Bretons, France	1	0	0	1	0
24	Corsicans, France	1	0	0	1	0
25	Friulians, Italy	1	0	1	1	1
26	Occitans, Italy	1	0	1	1	1
27	Basques, Spain	1	0	1	1	0
28	Catalans, Spain	1	0	1	1	0
29	Flemings, France	1	1	0	0	1
30	Walloons, Belgium	1	1	0	1	0
31	Swedes, Finland	1	1	1	0	0
32	South Tyroleans, Italy	1	1	1	0	0
33	Alsatians, France	1	1	1	1	1
34	Germans, Belgium	1	1	1	1	0
35	Flemings, Belgium	1	1	1	1	0

With 35 cases, this case study serves as a good example of the challenges of subjective assessment. Without some kind of tools to consolidate the data, it will be difficult to identify the core relationships between dependent and independent variables. Our first step, then, will be to apply information metrics to assess the four proposed factors X on an individual basis for their impact on the outcome variable Y. Table 7.2 shows the total $H(Y)$, conditional $H(Y|X)$, and mutual information $I(Y; X)$ metrics, as well as the direction of the relationships.

Table 7.2 Information Metrics for Ragin (1987) Politicized Ethnicity Data

	$H(Y)$	$H(Y|X)$	$I(Y; X)$	Direction
S	0.776	0.457	0.318	Positive
G	0.776	0.457	0.318	Positive
W	0.776	0.713	0.063	Positive
L	0.776	0.755	0.021	Positive

We can see in Table 7.2 that group size (S) and economic growth (G) are moderately informative about the politicization of ethnic minorities, while relative wealth (W) and linguistic abilities (L) are not very informative at all.

Our goal in drawing on QCA as a complement to information theory is to look at how these factors might combine to more strongly influence or reveal the outcome. Applying QCA, Ragin identifies four causal constellations:

$$E = LW + SG + Sw + lwG$$

QCA uses capital letters to indicate the presence of a factor and lowercase letters to indicate its absence. We can read these "prime implicants" as telling us that the outcome is most likely when linguistic ability (L) and relative wealth (W) are both present (LW), when group size (S) and economic growth (G) are both present (SG), when group size is present but relative wealth is absent (Sw), or when economic growth is present but relative wealth and linguistic ability are absent (lwG).

Three of these QCA "recipes" involve relative wealth (W) and linguistic ability (L), which we saw in our original information analysis were not, by themselves, very informative about the outcome. We can complement the QCA analysis by using information analysis to assess the information value of each of the combinations.

Since these are alternative pathways, the total information derived from these four composite factors can also be conceptualized as the logical union of the factors. That is, the outcome, ethnic political mobilization, is more likely if *any* of these composite factors is present. We can represent the four composite factors and their logical union (*ANY*) on a new truth table, as shown in Table 7.3.

Table 7.3 Truth Table for Prime Implicants of Ragin (1987) Ethnic Mobilization Data

Case	LW	SG	SW	lwG	ANY	Outcome
1	0	0	0	0	0	0
2	0	0	0	0	0	0

3	0	0	0	0	0	0
4	0	0	0	0	0	0
5	0	0	0	0	0	0
6	0	0	0	1	1	1
7	0	0	0	1	1	1
8	0	0	0	1	1	1
9	0	0	0	0	0	0
10	0	0	0	0	0	0
11	0	0	0	0	0	0
12	0	0	0	0	0	1
13	0	0	0	0	0	1
14	1	0	0	0	1	1
15	1	0	0	0	1	1
16	1	0	0	0	1	1
17	0	0	1	0	0	1
18	0	0	1	0	0	1
19	0	1	1	1	1	1
20	0	1	1	1	1	1
21	0	1	1	1	1	1
22	0	1	1	1	1	1
23	0	1	1	1	1	1
24	0	1	1	1	1	1
25	0	1	0	0	1	1
26	0	1	0	0	1	1
27	0	1	0	0	1	1
28	0	1	0	0	1	1
29	0	0	1	0	0	1
30	0	1	1	0	1	1
31	1	0	0	0	1	1
32	1	0	0	0	1	1
33	1	1	0	0	1	1
34	1	1	0	0	1	1
35	1	1	0	0	1	1

Significant leverage comes from applying the information metrics to this new truth table. In Table 7.4, we show the information results on each of these four combinations plus the logical union of the four composite conditions (ANY).

Table 7.4 reveals a number of interesting elements for the QCA analysis. First, on their own, none of the combinations are particularly informative. Indeed, group size (S) and economic growth (G) were both more informative by themselves (Table 7.2) than put together. Meanwhile, the SW, lwG, and LW combinations are only slightly more informative than L or W alone, but these factors are not very stable. Note that the direction of the relationship for language (L) and wealth (W) together flips to the opposite value of those two variables on their own. Although not very informative, it is also intriguing that economic growth reduces the likelihood of ethnic group political motivation when it is accompanied by the absence of language abilities (l) and the absence of a significant wealth differential (w).

The real power of combining QCA and information metrics is apparent when we consider the full QCA equation, which includes the logical union of the four composite variables (ANY). This composite data structure is more informative, $I(Y; X) = 0.418$, than were the individual factors or composite factors on their own. The combination of information metrics with QCA analysis helps us better understand the overall system of relationships within the data.

QCA and Information Metrics for Rokkan/Ragin Data on the Russian Revolution

A second data set analyzed by Ragin in his 1987 book comes from a study by Stein Rokkan (1970) on the effect of the Russian Revolution on working-class movements in other countries.

Table 7.4 Information Content of QCA Prime Implicants for Ragin (1987) Ethnic Mobilization Data

	$H(Y)$	$H(Y|X)$	$I(Y; X)$	Direction
ANY	0.78	0.36	0.42	Positive
SG	0.78	0.58	0.20	Positive
SW	0.78	0.65	0.13	Positive
lwG	0.78	0.67	0.11	Negative
LW	0.78	0.68	0.10	Negative

This table shows the information metrics for each of the QCA prime implicants and the combination of any of the patterns (ANY).

In some countries, the working-class movement was split by the Russian Revolution. Rokkan identifies four variables that could make such a split more likely: whether the state established a national church (vs. remained allied to the Roman Catholic church) (C), a significant role for Catholics in mass education (R), the state's willingness to protect landed interests (L), and whether the regime has been in place for a long time (E). The outcome (S) reflects a split in the working class after the Russian Revolution. Table 7.5 has the basic data.

We can begin with a straightforward information analysis of each of the four explanatory variables. This yields the mutual information scores shown in Table 7.6. Here we see that only a significant role for Catholics in mass education is very informative about the outcome, and even the information content of that variable is modest, at best. We can again turn to the combination of QCA and information methods to see if there are interesting combinations of these factors that are more informative about the outcome.

Table 7.5 Rokkan (1970)/Ragin (1987) Data on the Russian Revolution and Working-Class Movements in Europe

	C	R	L	E	S
Great Britain	1	0	1	1	0
Denmark	1	0	0	1	0
Sweden	1	0	0	1	0
Norway	1	0	0	0	1
Finland	1	0	0	0	1
Iceland	1	0	0	0	1
Germany	1	1	1	0	1
Netherland	1	1	0	1	0
Switzerland	1	1	0	1	0
Spain	0	0	1	1	1
France	0	0	0	1	1
Italy	0	0	0	0	1
Austria	0	1	1	0	0
Ireland	0	1	1	0	0
Belgium	0	1	0	0	0
Luxembourg	0	1	0	0	0

Table 7.6 Information Metrics for Rokkan (1970)/Ragin (1987) Data on the Russian Revolution and Working-Class Movements in Europe

	$H(Y)$	$H(Y|X)$	$I(Y; X)$	Direction
R	0.99	**0.78**	**0.21**	Negative
E	0.99	0.94	0.05	Negative
L	0.99	0.99	0.00	Negative
C	0.99	0.99	0.00	Negative

QCA analysis of this data set yields the three following sets of explanatory paths:

$$S = rle + crE + CRLe$$

The first of these tells us that a split in the worker's movement is more likely when the Catholic role in mass education is low/absent (r), the landed class is not protected by the state (l), and the state is relatively young (e). In the second scenario, a split is more likely when the state is officially aligned with Catholicism (c), Catholics don't play a role in mass education (r), and the state is relatively old (E). In the third scenario, a split is more likely when the other three factors are present (CRL) but the state is relatively young (e). This final scenario is particularly interesting because it switches the individual direction of influence of the other variables. That is, the presence of a protected landed class (L) makes a state with a national church (C), a high Catholic role in mass education (R), and a younger state (e) more likely to have a split in the workers' movement.

We can assess how informative these more complex QCA recipes are by calculating their entropy and mutual information scores. Again, we also include the *ANY* variable to represent the logical union of any of the composite factors. The entropy results for the Rokkan (1970)/ Ragin (1987) data are shown in Table 7.7.

Table 7.7 Information Content of QCA Prime Implicants for Rokkan (1970)/Ragin (1987) Data on the Russian Revolution and Working-Class Movements

	$H(Y)$	$H(Y|X)$	$I(Y; X)$	Direction
ANY	0.99	**0.29**	**0.70**	Positive
rle	0.99	0.61	0.38	Positive
crE	0.99	0.82	0.17	Positive
CRLe	0.99	0.91	0.08	Positive

Our strongest result, in this case, is again the total QCA equation. When we account for the possibility of any of the three pathways, the information score rises to nearly 0.70 of the original $H(Y) = 0.99$, indicating that ANY accounts for nearly 70% of the original uncertainty in the outcome variable. The most informative of the single factors was just 0.22. The increase to 0.70 is a substantial gain in information content.

In contrast to the Ragin (1987) data on ethnic political mobilization, in this study the more complex causal combinations are also more informative than was the finding with the single-variable relationships. While the Catholic role in mass education by itself had a mutual information score of 0.21 and a negative effect on the likelihood of a split in working-class movements, when we combine the absence of a Catholic role in mass education with the absence of state protection for the landed class, as well as a short regime duration, we improve the information content to 0.38.

The other QCA combinations still have relatively low information content. In particular, while the CRLe combination is conceptually interesting, it doesn't really tell us very much about the likelihood of a split in the working-class movement.

We can gain further leverage from the QCA–information connection by examining the reduction in uncertainty that comes from each additional element in a QCA recipe. To do this for the most informative rle recipe (no Catholic role in mass education, no state protection for the landed class, and a short regime duration), we break it into the three possible component permutations and then look at the information scores for each. These are shown in Table 7.8.

We can see in Table 7.8 that the heavy lifting for the rle combination comes entirely from the re pair, that is, the combination of the lack of a Catholic role in mass education and the short regime duration. The absence of state protection for the landed class (l) does not contribute any further information. This result is a new insight that enhances the QCA analysis.

Table 7.8 Information Content for QCA Component Parts of rle Recipe in Rokkan (1970)/Ragin (1987) Data on Working-Class Movements

	$H(Y)$	$H(Y|X)$	$I(Y; X)$	Direction
rle	0.99	0.61	0.38	Positive
re	0.99	0.61	0.38	Positive
rl	0.99	0.81	0.18	Positive
le	0.99	0.90	0.09	Positive

This table shows the relative information contribution of all of the possible subpairs that make up the rle *composite condition. The* re *pair by itself is just as informative as the* rle *triplet.*

QCA and Information Metrics for the Coercive Diplomacy Data

The two cases we have examined so far come from the fundamental QCA corpus. Another example that comes from outside that world is to return to our starting example of the George and Simons 1994 study of coercive diplomacy to see the leverage and nuance that can be provided by combining QCA and information theory. This study has just 7 cases, which is below the usual recommended minimum of 10, but that allows us to see the process a little more clearly.

We will start from Table 7.9, which reproduces Table 4.4 showing the basic truth table data for the coercive diplomacy study. We have rearranged the data to group the positive and negative outcomes. The QCA implicants are reasonably apparent here. In two out of three of the cases of successful coercive diplomacy, all of the factors are present, with the exception of *Domestic support,* which is present in the Cuba case but not in the Laos case. Meanwhile, the third successful case, Nicaragua, is clearly quite different, with only *Strong motivation* and *Strong leadership* to predict success.

This case is clearly what QCA analysis would call an "inconsistent case." In such instances, we see the way QCA analysts encourage a dialogue between the QCA results and the subjective, but expert, assessment of the case details. As already noted by our information analysis in Chapter 4, the Nicaragua case needs to be examined more carefully to determine whether it is appropriately grouped with the successful cases in this study. It may be that it simply identifies another path to outcome success. In this case, this path may be through the singularly critical role of strong leadership (note that strong motivation cannot really impress us since it exists in every case of both successful and unsuccessful outcomes). But it may also be that there is something fundamentally different about the Nicaragua case that makes it an inappropriate source for inference in this instance.

On the positive side—that is, the successful outcomes—if we discount the Nicaragua case, the only QCA recipe to predict success is the presence of all factors except for *Domestic support.* The QCA minimization rule tells us that we can combine the Laos and Cuba cases and drop the *Domestic support* variable. We can likewise drop the *Strong motivation* factor, which does not vary across any of the cases. Because there is no other variation, this formula cannot be further reduced.

We can assess the information content of this combined factor from the QCA truth table in Table 7.10. The overall uncertainty of Y is 0.99, while the uncertainty given this pattern of X values is 0.52, which means a reduction of uncertainty of 0.47. This is the same mutual information as we derived from the two most informative variables on their own: *Asymmetry of motivation* and *Clarity of terms.* This is as one would expect since they have exactly the same overall pattern across the cases.

Table 7.9 Truth Table for Coercive Diplomacy Study

	Clarity of Objective	Strong Motivation	Asymmetry of Motivation	Sense of Urgency	Strong Leadership	Domestic Support	International Support	Fear of Unacceptable Escalation	Clarity of Terms	Y: Success
Laos	1	1	1	1	1	0	1	1	1	1
Cuba	1	1	1	1	1	1	1	1	1	1
Nicaragua	0	1	0	0	1	0	0	0	0	1
Pearl Harbor	1	1	0	1	0	1	1	0	0	0
Vietnam	0	1	0	0	1	0	0	0	0	0
Libya	0	1	0	0	1	1	0	0	0	0
Persian Gulf	1	1	0	0	1	1	0	1	0	0

This table has been sorted to distinguish the successful and unsuccessful outcomes.

Remember, though, that QCA provides different results for predicting success or predicting failure. Running the failure analysis identifies three patterns that accord with failure. This, however, is not a very interesting result, since there are only four failure cases in the data. This means that each of these paths to failure is relatively unique. On the other hand, there is a core pattern that is common to all three of the failure recipes: strong motivation but with a lack of motivational symmetry, the presence of domestic support, and a lack of clarity in the terms. We can drop *Strong motivation,* which is irrelevant as a factor on either side since it is present in every case. This leaves those situations that have high domestic support but in which the terms are not clear and both sides are similarly motivated. This is identified in the variable alphabet used for QCA as *cFi*. That pattern is represented in the second to last column of independent variables in Table 7.10. We can see visually that it predicts three out of four failure cases, which yields a mutual information score $I(Y; X)$ of 0.52.

It is not our purpose to engage in an extensive or authoritative discussion of the coercive diplomacy results. But, it is worth noting where the combination of QCA and information analysis provides analytic leverage. In the first place, this combined analysis reemphasizes the strong role of *Clarity of terms* and *Asymmetry of motivation.* These two factors are exactly coterminous in these cases and also correspond perfectly with the QCA prime implicant for the positive results.

Table 7.10   QCA Truth Table for the Coercive Diplomacy Study

	A: Clarity of Objective	B: Strong Motivation	C: Asymmetry of Motivation	D: Sense of Urgency	E: Strong Leadership	F: Domestic Support	G: International Support	H: Fear of Unacceptable Escalation	I: Clarity of Terms	cFi	All Factors Except Public Support	Y: Success
Pearl Harbor	1	1	0	1	0	1	1	0	0	1	0	0
Laos	1	1	1	1	1	0	1	1	1	0	1	1
Cuba	1	1	1	1	1	1	1	1	1	0	1	1
Vietnam	0	1	0	0	1	0	0	0	0	0	0	0
Libya	0	1	0	0	1	1	0	0	0	1	0	0
Nicaragua	0	1	0	0	1	0	0	0	0	0	0	1
Persian Gulf	1	1	0	0	1	1	0	1	0	1	0	0

Likewise, the largely negative relationship between domestic public support and success is a remarkable finding that is not highlighted in the original analysis. This could, of course, be a quirk of the cases, but it is also possible that strong public support has pushed American decision makers to take actions that might be riskier and that they would otherwise choose to avoid.

The QCA process emphasizes the interaction of a more systematic analytical approach with the nuanced and in-depth reading of the case material. To really follow through on the QCA connection with the information method would require returning to the case details to assess whether these results point to areas for more careful assessment of the cases or the variables. In particular, we have highlighted the unique dimensions of the Nicaragua case, which surely merits some more in-depth study.

Conclusion

Thiem and Duşa (2013) assert that "Qualitative Comparative Analysis (QCA) counts among the most important methodological innovations social science methodology has witnessed in the past two decades" (p. 1). QCA is a particularly useful complement to the information theory approach because it has a strongly worked-out philosophy of small-*n* interpretation that understands both the nuance of case analysis and the importance of a systematic approach. As we have shown in this chapter, QCA and information theory can be combined to significantly improve the power of both. QCA enhances information analytics by reducing the number of independent variables to be analyzed and by characterizing the relationships between the original variables. Information theory enhances QCA by providing a metric for understanding the information content in each set of grouped factors. Comparative case study findings and implications benefit from both, complementing the qualitative analysis toolkit and the knowledge produced from case study research.

SELECTED INTRODUCTORY QCA RESOURCES

Legewie, N. (2013). An introduction to applied data analysis with qualitative comparative analysis (QCA). *Forum: Qualitative Social Research (FQS)*, 14(3), Art. 15. Available from http://www.qualitative-research.net/index.php/fqs/article/view/1961/3594

Ragin, C. (1987). *The comparative method: Moving beyond qualitative and quantitative strategies*. Berkeley: University of California Press.

Ragin, C. (2008). *Redesigning social inquiry: Fuzzy sets and beyond*. Chicago, IL: University of Chicago Press.

Rihoux, B., & Ragin, C. (2008). *Configurational comparative methods: Qualitative Comparative Analysis (QCA) and related techniques*. Thousand Oaks, CA: Sage.

Schneider, C. Q., & Wagemann, C. (2012). *Set-theoretic methods for the social sciences: A guide to qualitative comparative analysis*. Cambridge, England: Cambridge University Press.

Thiem, A., & Duşa, A. (2013). *Qualitative comparative analysis with R: A user's guide*. New York, NY: Springer.

QCA SOFTWARE AND WEB RESOURCES

Compasss. A web page for comparative case research resources. www.compasss.org.

Duşa, A., & Thiem, A. (2014). QCA: A package for qualitative comparative analysis, Version 1.1-3 (R Package). Available from http://cran.r-project.org/web/packages/QCA/index.html

Longest, K. C., & Vaisey, S. (2008). fuzzy: A program for performing qualitative comparative analyses (QCA) in Stata. *Stata Journal, 8*(1), 79–104.

Ragin, C., & Davey, S. (2014). fs/QCA [Computer program], Version 2.5. Irvine: University of California, Irvine.

Ragin, C., Drass, K. A., & Davey, S. (2006). *Fuzzy-set/Qualitative Comparative Analysis 2.0*. Tucson: Department of Sociology, University of Arizona. Available from http://www.u.arizona.edu/~cragin/fsQCA/

Additional resources are provided at http://study.sagepub.com/drozdova.

CHAPTER

8

Conclusion

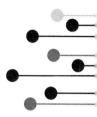

The Information Revolution was sparked by Claude Shannon's articulation of a quantitative approach to understanding information. The underlying intuition was that all information could be conceptualized as discrete units, as bits, that with the appropriate channel size could be transmitted essentially without error. Neuroscientist and statistician Liam Paninski (2013) has called information theory "a pinnacle of statistical research . . . at once beautiful and applicable to a remarkably wide variety of questions" (p. 1191). Indeed, information theory has been applied across a range of fields and has proven a powerful tool for many different kinds of problems. In this book, we have demonstrated that Shannon's insights about quantifying communication and measuring uncertainty and complexity are directly applicable to the challenges of rigorously and systematically assessing the information content of comparative case studies.

Somewhat ironically, the emerging era of big data has been accompanied by a heightened interest in small-*n* methods. The more distant and abstract our data become, the more there is a need for meaningful theory to guide the analysis of data, as well as the kind of validation and the different quality of insights that can be gained from the nuanced and hands-on detail of small-*n* work. The increasing computational power sitting on our desks, and even in our pockets, does not diminish the traditional benefits of case study work for hypothesis generation and for teasing out complex causality. At the same time, the interest in case study work has heightened for the many analysts whose primary interest may be more in gaining subject area expertise than in mastering the increasingly rarefied technical skills required for computational statistics.

Building on a rich and growing tradition of multimethod scholarship, we have argued that having a variety of complementary research methods and analytical tools benefits the goals of advancing and strengthening human knowledge as well as improving judgment under uncertainty. Case studies bring important nuances and depth of understanding that are especially valued in policy-relevant work, where the analytical insights gained through advanced methods must typically be related in a straightforward way to various practical problems and explained to multidisciplinary or nontechnical audiences. A rigorous qualitative understanding of the problems complemented by objective metrics that are accurate as well as straightforward and effective in communicating the knowledge gained from complex information is often essential for both scientific and practical impact.

The renewed interest in comparative case studies has led to a more careful discussion and working out of the basic scientific and philosophical principles of case study analysis and a flowering of new approaches and techniques. We developed our information-theoretic approach as an effective and appropriate complement to this movement toward more rigorous and systematic comparative case study work. The application of information theory to case study work can both discipline the case study process and provide conceptually straightforward metrics for a clearer understanding of the relationships between factors and outcomes in small-n work. Information metrics can be calculated with only a minimal set of quantitative tools.

These information-theoretic tools use a very accessible set of principles that we have reviewed and explained hands-on in this book. The insights generated by the application of information metrics to case study findings can be profound and are complementary to the extant benefits of case methods. The insights of information theory in no way reduce the value of qualitative work; they augment the findings by going beyond what is typically achieved in simply eyeballing or subjectively assessing the comparative results, as has often been the practice in case study research.

In contrast to more traditional statistical measures, these information metrics are fundamentally nonparametric and do not degrade in the context of low observation numbers. Rather than being an estimator or abstract statistical concept, Shannon's notion of mutual information is a precise measure of how informative one variable can be about another. This notion of information has an intuitive meaning that is particularly appropriate for our digital era.

Information, Research, and the Digital Era

Our central argument has been that information theory offers a way to significantly improve small-n analysis. This does not need to come at the expense of the traditional strengths of comparative case analysis—the ability to directly observe nuance and trace the causal processes through a more detailed and context-aware analysis (George & Bennett, 2005). Instead, the techniques we have presented provide an additional tool that can make small-n analysis more rigorous and systematic.

The information theory approach to comparative case studies builds an eminently appropriate metric that allows us to precisely understand the amount of information about an outcome that is contained in an explanatory factor. This metric has a number of appealing properties:

- The information metric is *objective and intuitive*. It aligns with our fundamental research question, which is the following: How much does knowing the value of X contribute to knowing the value of Y? Extracting information from cases is the basic purpose of case study analysis. A measure of how much information is contained in the cases makes perfect sense for this role. Our reproducible measure enables more rigorous comparisons of results across cases, a useful addition to the qualitative toolbox.

- The information metric is *easy to interpret*. It varies between 0, where knowing the value of X contributes nothing to our knowledge of Y, and 1, where knowing the value of X is perfectly informative about the value of Y. Perfect uncertainty, where there is a 50/50 chance of Y being either 0 or 1, is at the halfway mark. Naturally, we want to find Xs that will be relatively more informative about Y. This scale makes for an intuitive, broadly applicable, and easy to use metric. It is consistent with how many people think about the world in terms of probability or chances, and for those who do not think this way, it is nevertheless intuitive and straightforward.

- The information metric is very *straightforward to calculate*. Mostly this calculation requires the ability to count. It is true that the same fingers used for counting have to be able to use the log function on a calculator or, even better, in a spreadsheet. But as we have shown, these calculations are very easy to do. In Appendix A and on the website that accompanies this book, we provide the Excel spreadsheet formulas for conducting this analysis.

- The information metric is *nonparametric*. It makes no assumptions about underlying distributions or probabilities. This is particularly important for small-n analysis, where probability distributions can be very complex or unknown and where traditional statistical tools break down. Information-theoretic measures can identify relationships where more traditional statistical measures, such as those based on central tendencies, may fall short or prove inapplicable. A mutual information value of zero will precisely indicate that the values of a particular X variable in the examined cases are completely noninformative about values of the outcome variable, whereas a nonzero result will detect underlying dependencies in complex variable interactions.

- Along these same lines, the information metric is *not an estimator*. Within a given set of cases, it provides a precise measurement of how much knowledge we gain about Y from knowing X. This is parallel to information theory's role in understanding digital data compression. We know, again from information theory, exactly how pixilated a digital photograph will be when it is stored as a 1-kilobyte, 100-kilobyte, or 1,000-kilobyte file. So, too, information theory can tell us how much resolution we can get on the outcome variable from our set of explanatory factors.

- The information metric *separates signal from noise* in qualitative findings. Information theory emerged to rigorously and elegantly answer the fundamental questions of how information can be accurately identified in a noisy world. In this regard, the notions of information uncertainty (or entropy) are essentially the same across a broad range of real-world problems: from deciding whether your system is cyber-secure, when to sell a stock, or how much intelligence is enough to what happens when a black hole swallows a star, or how much food will feed the hungry. Stemming from the all too familiar challenge of separating signal from noise, our information analytics extend these capabilities into the new domains of qualitative knowledge.

- The information metric contributes to a better *synthesis of the multimethod insights* from the diverse data increasingly required to solve complex problems. Sophisticated computational tools have been advanced for analyzing massive amounts of digital data, but challenges remain in areas such as the effective analysis of data from asymmetric sources or in different formats that do not easily combine. Information analysis provides meaningful, comparable measures regardless of the underlying inputs. It combines naturally with other context-specific approaches to inform advanced data analytics with relevant theory and qualitative subject matter expertise to improve policy or operational decisions in complex situations under high uncertainty and costs. This simple metric is a sensible and intuitive extension of information theory, a well-established and rich intellectual tradition that sparked the Information Revolution and continues to generate new ideas and applications across a broad range of fields.

By itself, the information metric gives us a rigorous and reproducible assessment of the individual relationship between each independent variable and the dependent variable. It does not tell us about how the independent variables might work together to improve our knowledge of the outcome. For this purpose, we demonstrated in Chapter 7 that information metrics can be combined with the power of qualitative case analysis (QCA) to provide a better understanding of how explanatory factors might be combined to express more complex causal relationships within the given data.

The QCA connection puts the researcher in touch with a very well-worked-out logic for rigorous and careful case study analysis. With QCA and information metrics, we can enhance the single-variable analysis to see the different patterns in which the explanatory factors might combine to influence the outcome. QCA alone can only identify the patterns. It is significantly strengthened with the addition of information metrics to gain insights into how informative each alternative pattern is about the outcome variable and to assess the improvement in information provided by each additional variable in a QCA recipe.

Reducing Uncertainty and Improving Judgment: Using Information Analysis in the Real World

Throughout this book, we have argued that information theory can be of particular use to policy makers and others who have to make consequential decisions facing complex problems in an environment of uncertainty. Both information theory and the logic of structured-focused comparison grew out of the Cold War needs to improve intelligence and decision making in the shadow of thermonuclear war. Those challenges are still with us in the Information Age but are now also compounded with additional risks ranging from cyber-war to low-tech terrorism or hybrid threats. Amazing technological advances have helped humanity move forward, but they have not removed the basic human challenges of character and judgment, as well as the necessity to make sense of information and act on it effectively.

Policy makers and business leaders need tools to help them interpret and understand the real world. Their essential problem comes from both too much and too little information that usually has to be assessed in a context with significant time pressure. Especially in the world of big data, complex policy issues involve huge flows of information, much of which is just noise. At the same time, decisions often have to be made without all of the desired information in hand. Understanding which factors are most informative can be a key to better quality as well as more efficient decision making in this difficult environment.

Policy makers and others who need to make decisions have always been attracted to the case study approach as an accessible and concrete way to understand the likely consequences of their decisions and to develop a consensus about lessons learned and best practices. The information-theoretic techniques we have introduced here are highly complementary to these needs. Information metrics are straightforward to calculate and are sufficiently intuitive to serve in a practical real-world context.

The Limits and Further Possibilities for Information Analysis

Of course, information-theoretic metrics are not magic. They can significantly improve case study analysis. They can help us better understand and interpret the relationships between a set of independent variables and a dependent variable. But, as we emphasized in Chapter 6, these methods cannot solve all of the challenges of drawing inference from small samples. Even if we were somehow confident that our cases were randomly drawn, the basic constraints of small n still hold and require appropriate analytic methods to draw valid conclusions. Without a decent-sized sample, standard errors will be large and inferential confidence will be limited from a statistical perspective. And, of course, small-n case studies can rarely make the random claim with very much confidence. But typically, case study research does not make statistical claims; it is designed explicitly for different sorts of valuable inferences and insights.

For these purposes, it is imperative that comparative case studies be designed and conducted with a high level of intentionality and awareness of the case selection process. How you choose your cases has a direct effect on how you draw inferences from them. If you have good reasons to believe that your cases are effective representatives of a larger universe of cases (i.e., appropriate instances of a particular phenomenon), the inference process is relatively straightforward. Information metrics strengthen these kinds of studies by providing a clearer picture of the relationship between factors and outcomes in the cases. The concept of reducing uncertainty about outcomes translates directly into clear inferential expectations.

As we argued in Chapter 3, even case sets with known biases can provide strong inferential leverage. The logic of most-likely and least-likely cases emphasizes that cases with known biases can provide stronger evidence for confirming or infirming a hypothesis than random cases (Eckstein, 1975; Lijphart, 1971). The important thing is to be intentional about the relationship between the cases and the larger class of things about which one wishes to draw inferences and to effectively articulate the rationale, logic, and evidence supporting the study's design and conclusions.

Analysts will always make inferences from cases. That is why they are called analysts and why they are called cases. Analysts are trying to figure out the world, and by definition, cases are instances of some larger phenomenon of interest (Ragin & Becker, 1992). Our argument is that the process of inference should be disciplined and careful. Information metrics can help ensure that the content of the cases is systematically evaluated and appropriately understood. The use of information analytics also forces the analyst to organize and present the data in a systematic and replicable fashion. Results provide end users—whether analysts, scholars, policy makers, or other practitioners—with concrete objective measures of the information content and relative uncertainty measures of the findings drawn from those cases.

We should also say a word here about the merits of mixed methods. Across many fields, the late 20th century was a methodological battleground pitting the advocates of case analysis, fieldwork, and deep subject knowledge against those carrying the banner for the computational revolution and its burgeoning array of shiny new quantitative tools. By the start of the 21st century, this conflict had largely given way to the eminently reasonable notion that there were benefits to both approaches. This, in turn, has elevated the concept of mixed methods, the idea that research problems could be profitably addressed with a range of complementary and cross-reinforcing methodological tools.

So, too, we contribute information metrics as a complement to both of these traditional approaches. It is neither a replacement for deep immersion in a small set of comparative cases nor for the large-N methods of inference from quantitative analysis. It is an additional tool that can help bridge this gap by providing a more rigorous and systematic understanding of the content of small-n studies.

The information theory approach is also a natural methodology for the increasingly popular conduct of meta-analysis. As the body of research continues to grow exponentially, and especially as the studies become easily accessible in a digital and searchable format, there is increasing leverage to be derived from combining the results of multiple studies, as exemplified by the Rudel (2005) study of rainforests we examined in Chapter 5. Information theory can significantly improve the prospects for combining studies by disciplining the way study results are organized and presented. Information content can be integrated across multiple studies and, as we have argued throughout this book, conceptually captures the essential thing we are looking for from these meta-efforts: information and knowledge.

Extensions

For a number of reasons, both practical and theoretical, we have limited our discussion to data with binary {0, 1} coding. This approach is consistent with the original formulation of the method of structured-focused comparison articulated by Alexander George, as well as Charles Ragin's method of crisp-set QCA (csQCA) that we discussed in Chapter 7. Binary coding makes the pattern of case results easier to see visually and also facilitates a focus on critical dichotomies in the coding of complex variables and the very straightforward use of information theory as we have presented it here.

It is important to note, however, that these same concepts can also be applied to data with multilevel and even continuous outcomes as well as variable sequences or other combinatorics. Shannon's information theory is built on the fundamental insight that all information could be conceptualized and transmitted as binary data, which is how the ones and zeros streaming across the Internet become furry creature pictures on your phone. Nonetheless, we have proposed starting with binary coding as the most mathematically tractable and accessible for a broad range of policy makers and qualitative researchers.

In Chapter 7, we connected information analysis to the strong body of work on QCA for the purposes of understanding the interaction of independent variables. Most of the core information techniques we have discussed have focused on the bivariate relationships between individual explanatory factors and outcomes. But there is much more room to explore ways in which information metrics can be used to describe both the relationships between explanatory factors and how informative they are about an outcome. Looking at the multivariate information structures will provide an additional level of analysis, although, of course, at some cost in complexity and mathematical accessibility.

Finally, there are significant potential benefits in working through the connections between information theory and the rapidly growing world of Bayesian statistics. The Bayesian emphasis on probability as a state of knowledge connects directly to the notion of information (Jaynes, 1986). Indeed, Adom Giffin (2008) argues that Bayes's rule is a special case of maximum entropy updating and demonstrates the underlying mathematical compatibility of Bayesian and entropy methods.

Conclusion

Comparative case studies have retained and even gained relevance despite the ascendance of big data. The developing understanding of the inferential potential of small-n study, along with its many demonstrated benefits, has significantly increased the interest in more rigorous and systematic approaches to case study work.

Information theory provides a mathematically powerful but easy to calculate and intuitively straightforward set of metrics for enhancing comparative case studies. Information theory complements qualitative analysis. It disciplines the analysis and its presentation, without diminishing the benefits that arise from the more nuanced and detailed understandings that small-n comparative case studies can provide. It is the right metric for quantifying qualitative analysis in the Information Age and beyond.

Additional resources are provided at http://study.sagepub.com/drozdova.

APPENDIX

A

Using Excel for Information Metrics

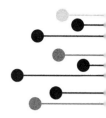

Throughout this book, we have emphasized that doing the information metrics calculations is exceedingly straightforward. They can certainly be done by hand, but it will likely be easier to do them with Excel or a similar spreadsheet program. We also provide, in Appendix B, the code for automating the entropy and mutual information calculations with the R statistical program.

Step 1: Enter Data

Step 1 with Excel is to enter your data. You may already have the data somewhere else, in which case you can just cut and paste. Alternatively, one of the benefits of small *n* is that it probably isn't that much of a burden to put the data in by hand. In either case, the data need to be all binary {0, 1}. The variables should be in columns, with the observations in rows. Figure A.1 is a screenshot showing the data block in cells B2 to K8 based on *The Limits of Coercive Diplomacy* (George & Simons, 1994) data from the example in Chapter 4.

	A	B	C	D	E	F	G	H	I	J	K
		X1	X2	X3	X4	X5	X6	X7	X8	X9	Y
1		Objective	Motivation	Asymmetr	Urgency	Leadership	Domestic	Intl	Escalation	Terms	Success
2	Pearl Harbor	1	1	0	1	0	1	1	0	0	0
3	Laos	1	1	1	1	1	0	1	1	1	1
4	Cuba	1	1	1	1	1	1	1	1	1	1
5	Vietnam	0	1	0	0	1	0	0	0	0	0
6	Libya	0	1	0	0	1	1	0	0	0	0
7	Nicaragua	0	1	0	0	1	0	0	0	0	1
8	Persian Gulf	1	1	0	0	1	1	0	1	0	0
9											
10											
11											
12											
13											
14											
15											
16											
17											

Figure A.1   Data Entry in Excel

Step 2: Probability Calculations

All of the entropy statistics can be quickly calculated from the joint probabilities using the *abcd* shortcut, as discussed in Chapter 2. These four letters refer to the four cells of a 2 × 2 table (see Table A.1) indicating the percentage of the data in each quadrant (the joint probabilities).

Table A.1   Joint Probabilities

	$X = 1$	$X = 0$
$Y = 1$	a	b
$Y = 0$	c	d

The *abcd* values can be calculated in four rows below the raw data. For this purpose, you will also need to know *n*, which is just the number of observations (the number of cases).

a is the count of the number of observations where $X = 1$ and $Y = 1$ divided by *n*. You could easily do this by hand, or you could use an Excel formula, which is the way we will show here.

For this example, we will suppose that your data are in the block defined by B2 to K8, as shown in Figure A.1. This would imply 10 variables (column B to column K) and 7 cases (row 2 to row 8, inclusive). Your dependent (outcome) variable needs to be in the last column (in this example, column K). The formula for *a*, written here for the variable in column B, counts the number of times that variable is 1 at the same time that the dependent variable (column K) is 1. This number is then divided by the total number of cases, which we can get just by counting up the number of rows. We use the dollar signs in front of the row and column identifiers for the dependent variable because we want those to stay constant as we copy the formula to other columns or rows. We do the same thing for just the row numbers for the independent variable to keep those constant when we copy the formula for the *bcd* calculations.

```
=countifs (B$2:B$8, "=1", $K$2:$K$8, "=1") /
     count (B$2:B$8)
```

You then need to copy this formula across the row for the other independent variable columns (in this example, columns C through J). The easy way to do this is with what is often called "the Magic Black Box" but which Microsoft calls the "Fill Handle." This is the small black square on the bottom right of a selected cell. Click on the cell, then click and drag the Fill Handle to copy the formula from cell B2 all the way over to cell J2, that is, for all of the independent variables. The independent variable column locators in the formula will automatically change. The dependent variable locators, which we protected with the dollar signs ($), will remain the same, as they should.

Next you need to copy this same approach for the *bcd* rows. Here are all four formulas for the B column. Use the Fill Handle to copy these formulas for all of the independent variables.

a: = countifs (B\$2:B\$8, "=1", \$K\$2:\$K\$8, "=1")/
count(B\$2:B\$8)

b: = countifs (B\$2:B\$8, "=0", \$K\$2:\$K\$8, "=1")/
count(B\$2:B\$8)

c: = countifs (B\$2:B\$8, "=1", \$K\$2:\$K\$8, "=0")/
count(B\$2:B\$8)

d: = countifs (B\$2:B\$8, "=0", \$K\$2:\$K\$8, "=0")/
count(B\$2:B\$8)

Figure A.2 shows what it will look like for this example.

One additional trick (discussed in Chapters 2 and 4) is that if any of these values are zero, we need to approximate them by a small number to make sure that the logs are defined. Just change them from zero to 0.00001. This adjustment makes no substantive difference but enables us to calculate the information metrics despite zero counts for some of the factor-outcome combinations. If you count yourself a real Excel wiz, you could use an =if() function to automate that, but for most people, it won't be too onerous to do that step by hand.

We now have everything we need to do all of the information calculations.

	A	B	C	D	E	F	G	H	I	J	K	L
		X1	X2	X3	X4	X5	X6	X7	X8	X9	Y	
1		Objective	Motivation	Asymmetry	Urgency	Leadership	Domestic	Intl	Escalation	Terms	Success	
2	Pearl Harbor	1	1	0	1	0	1	1	0	0	0	
3	Laos	1	1	1	1	1	0	1	1	1	1	
4	Cuba	1	1	1	1	1	1	1	1	1	1	
5	Vietnam	0	1	0	0	1	0	0	0	0	0	
6	Libya	0	1	0	0	1	1	0	0	0	0	
7	Nicaragua	0	1	0	0	1	0	0	0	0	1	
8	Persian Gulf	1	1	0	0	1	1	0	1	0	0	
9												
10	a	0.286	0.429	0.286	0.286	0.429	0.143	0.286	0.286	0.286		
11	b	0.143	0.000	0.143	0.143	0.000	0.286	0.143	0.143	0.143		
12	c	0.286	0.571	0.000	0.143	0.429	0.429	0.143	0.143	0.000		
13	d	0.286	0.000	0.571	0.429	0.143	0.143	0.429	0.429	0.571		

Figure A.2   Excel Worksheet With Calculated *abcd* Values

Step 3: Entropy and Mutual Information Metrics

We need three different entropy metrics, which build on each other. The first is $H(Y)$, which is just the total entropy of Y. That gives us our baseline uncertainty about whether Y is 1 or 0. The second is $H(Y|X)$, which is the entropy of Y conditional on X. That tells us how uncertain we are about whether Y is 0 or 1, given that we know the value of X. The third is the mutual information $I(Y; X)$, or uncertainty reduction, which is just the difference between $H(Y)$ and $H(Y|X)$. In other words, how much more information do we gain about Y knowing X compared to not knowing X?

Again, we can calculate each of these quantities from the *abcd* values. These formulas are set out below, in each case starting with the mathematical formula and then showing the Excel version. Following the example started earlier, we will assume that *abcd* are in rows 10, 11, 12, and 13, respectively. Obviously, you'll have to adjust this to whatever rows your *abcd* calculations are in. We show the formula for the variable in the B column. As with the calculations of *abcd,* you can use the Fill Handle to copy these formulas to the other dependent variables with the correct adjustments made automatically.

$$H(Y) = -(c + d) \log_2 (c + d) - (a + b) \log_2 (a + b)$$

$$= - (\text{B12} + \text{B13}) * \text{LOG} (\text{B12} + \text{B13, 2})$$

$$- (\text{B10} + \text{B11}) * \text{LOG} (\text{B10} + \text{B11, 2})$$

$$H(Y|X) = - [d (\log_2 (d) - \log_2 (b + d)) + b (\log_2 (b) - \log_2 (b + d))]$$

$$- [c (\log_2 (c) - \log_2 (a + c)) + a (\log_2 (a) - \log_2 (a + c))]$$

$$= - (\text{B13} * (\text{LOG} (\text{B13, 2}) - \text{LOG} (\text{B11} + \text{B13, 2}))$$

$$+ \text{B11} * (\text{LOG} (\text{B11, 2}) - \text{LOG} (\text{B11} + \text{B13, 2})))$$

$$- (\text{B12} * (\text{LOG} (\text{B12, 2}) - \text{LOG} (\text{B10} + \text{B12, 2}))$$

$$+ \text{B10} * (\text{LOG} (\text{B10, 2}) - \text{LOG} (\text{B10} + \text{B12, 2})))$$

To calculate the mutual information $I(Y; X)$, just subtract $H(Y|X)$ from $H(Y)$. This tells us, for each of the independent variables X, how knowing X reduces the uncertainty about Y. With Excel, you can just subtract the cell holding $H(Y|X)$ from the cell with $H(Y)$:

$$I(Y; X) = H(Y) - H(Y|X)$$

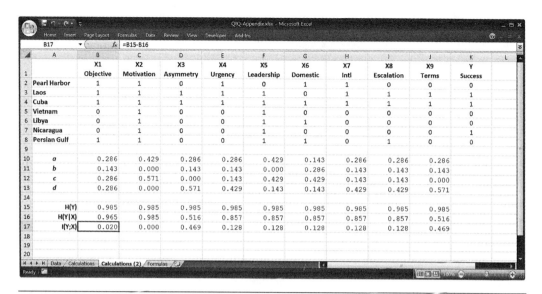

Figure A.3 Screenshot of Excel for $I(Y; X)$ Calculations

Figure A.3 shows the completed calculations in Excel.

That's it. If you want to make it even easier, you can just go to http://study.sagepub.com/drozdova and copy our Excel spreadsheet that contains all of these formulas. Make the appropriate changes for the number of variables and cases in your study and you are done.

Alternatively, if you are interested in automating the process further, you can turn to the free statistical software R and the routine in Appendix B.

Using R for Information Metrics

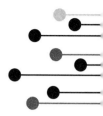

R is a powerful computer language for doing statistics. It has a somewhat steep learning curve but is rapidly becoming the language of choice for data analysts. You can freely download R from www.cran.org. The RStudio R interface and editor, from rstudio.org, is also highly recommended. There are a number of resources for learning R, but for obvious reasons, we are partial to *A Survivor's Guide to R* (Gaubatz, 2015).

R can be very effectively integrated into qualitative data work. The RQDA package, for example, provides text mining capabilities and the ability to derive quantitative concept scales that are organized around qualitative cases (Huang, 2014). As discussed at the end of Chapter 7, there are also very helpful R packages to facilitate qualitative case analysis (QCA) methods.

We provide here the core of an R routine for doing entropy and mutual information calculations. A more extensive version, along with all of the code and routines used in this book (including the QCA procedures), can be downloaded from http://study.sagepub.com/drozdova.

We provide two stand-alone functions here. The first uses conditional and joint probabilities and calculates entropy scores for a complete data set. The second demonstrates the *abcd* method from Chapter 2 and calculates the information metrics between any two variables.

Example 1: Deriving Information Metrics From Conditional Probabilities

The following example presents the code for an R function to use the total, joint, and conditional probabilities to calculate the information metrics. The function takes as its input a data set and outputs a table of results.

(Using all probability values)

```
# ===== Entropy Function to perform information analysis =======
# Input is a dataframe of independent variables with the
# dependent variable in the last column. Variable names are
# in the first row. Case names are in the first column.
# All values must be {0, 1}.
#
# To streamline some of the calculations, we set up an inverted
# copy of the data set switching 0/1 in the dataframe edat2.

entropy = function(edata){

  edat1 = edata                      # Copy data w/o case names
  edat2 = abs(edat1 - 1)             # Copy w/inverted 0's/1's
  out1 = edat1[dim(edat1)[2]]        # Y variable for outcomes
  out2 = edat2[dim(edat2)[2]]        # Inverted Y variable
  edat1 = edat1[-dim(edat1)[2]]      # X variables alone
  edat2 = edat2[-dim(edat2)[2]]      # Inverted X variables
  n = dim(edat1)[1]                  # Get number of cases


  # ===== Joint Probabilities =====================================
  # The joint probabilities are the number of times the two
  # values occur divided by the total number of cases.

  jp00 = sapply(edat2*out2[,1], sum)/n # Joint pr x=0 & y=0
  jp11 = sapply(edat1*out1[,1], sum)/n # Joint pr x=1 & y=1
  jp01 = sapply(edat2*out1[,1], sum)/n # Joint pr x=0 & y=1
  jp10 = sapply(edat1*out2[,1], sum)/n # Joint pr x=1 & y=0

  # ===== Total Probabilities for each Attribute ================
  # The total probability that x=0 is the sum of the joint
  # probabilities of x=0 when y=0 and x=0 when y=1 etc.

  tp0 = jp00 + jp01                  # Total probability x=0
  tp1 = jp11 + jp10                  # Total probability x=1


  # ===== Conditional Probabilities ===============================
  # The conditional probability is the probability that y is a
  # specific value given that x is a specific value.

  cp00 = jp00/tp0                    # Cond pr y=0 given x=0
  cp01 = jp10/tp1                    # Cond pr y=0 given x=1
  cp10 = jp01/tp0                    # Cond pr y=1 given x=0
  cp11 = jp11/tp1                    # Cond pr y=1 given x=1
```

```
# ===== NA Substitutions =======================================
# Where probabilities or logs are undefined, replace with 0
# since as X approaches zero, xlogx approaches 0.

cp00 = ifelse(is.na(cp00), 0, cp00)   # Change NA to 0
cp01 = ifelse(is.na(cp01), 0, cp01)
cp10 = ifelse(is.na(cp10), 0, cp10)
cp11 = ifelse(is.na(cp11), 0, cp11)


# Approximate 0's by .00001 to keep logs defined

cp00 = ifelse(cp00 == 0, .00001, cp00)
cp01 = ifelse(cp01 == 0, .00001, cp01)
cp10 = ifelse(cp10 == 0, .00001, cp10)
cp11 = ifelse(cp11 == 0, .00001, cp11)


# ===== Conditional Information Entropy ====================
H = -tp0 * (cp00 * log2(cp00) +       # Conditional Entropy for
     cp10 * log2(cp10)) -             #   for outcome Y given X.
     tp1 * (cp01 * log2(cp01) +
     cp11 * log2(cp11))


# ===== Mutual Information -- I(Y;X)============================
# (uncertainty reduction in outcome Y due to X)

pY0 = sum(out2)/n                     # Total probability Y=0
pY1 = sum(out1)/n                     # Total probability Y=1
HY  = -pY0 * log2(pY0) -             # Outcome uncertainty of Y
     pY1 * log2(pY1)

MI = HY-H                             # Mutual Information

# ===== Create a variable to record direction of relationship
# (positive or negative)

D = ifelse(jp00 + jp11 > jp01 + jp10, 1, -1)

Hout = cbind(HY, H, MI, D)            # Output Total Entropy,
return(Hout)                          #   Cond Entropy, Mutual
                                      #   Information, direction
}                                     # End of Entropy Function
```

R Code to Perform Information Analysis

Example 2: Deriving Information Metrics With the *abcd* Method

This function uses the shortcut *abcd* method from Chapter 2 that was also used in Appendix A for the Excel calculations. *abcd* are the proportions of the data that fall in each cell of a 2 × 2 table (the joint probabilities). While the function in Example 1 calculates the information metrics for an entire data set, this function, entropy2, calculates the metrics for just two variables *X* and *Y* at a time.

```
# ================================================================
# This is another version of the entropy function that uses the
# abcd method and computes entropy scores for any two variables.
# Both variables have to be binary {0, 1} and have the same
# number of observations.

entropy2 = function(x, y){

  if(length(x) != length(y)){             # Error checking
    warning("X and Y must have same length")
    print(paste("Length of X = ", length(x)))
    print(paste("Length of Y = ", length(y)))
    stop()                                 # Exit function if X
    }                                      #  and Y lengths differ

  n = length(x)                            # Set number of cases

  # ===== Joint Probabilities ====================================
  # The joint probabilities are the number of times the two
  # values occur divided by the total number of cases.
  # We will set this up as the following matrix:
  #
  #          X
  #         1 0
  #   Y = 1  a b
  #       0  c d
  #
  a = sum(x * y)/n                         # Joint pr x=1 & y=1
  b = sum((!x) * y)/n                      # Joint pr x=0 & y=1
  c = sum(x * (!y))/n                      # Joint pr x=1 & y=0
  d = sum((!x) * (!y))/n                   # Joint pr x=0 & y=0

  # ===== NA Substitutions =======================================
  # Where probabilities or logs are undefined, replace with 0
  # since as x approaches zero, xlogx approaches 0.
```

```
a = ifelse(is.na(a), 0, a)                # Change NA to 0
b = ifelse(is.na(b), 0, b)
c = ifelse(is.na(c), 0, c)
d = ifelse(is.na(d), 0, d)


# Approximate 0's by .00001 to keep logs defined

a = ifelse(a == 0, .00001, a)
b = ifelse(b == 0, .00001, b)
c = ifelse(c == 0, .00001, c)
d = ifelse(d == 0, .00001, d)


# ===== Conditional Information Entropy ========================
HYgX = -(d * (log2(d) - log2(b + d)) +
         b * (log2(b) - log2(b + d))) -
        (c * (log2(c) - log2(a + c)) +
         a * (log2(a) - log2(a + c)))

# This is an algebraically streamlined version of:
#   HYgX = - (b + d) * ((d/(b + d)) * log2(d/(b + d))
#                     + (b/(b + d)) * log2(b/(b + d)))
#          - (a + c) * ((c/(a + c)) * log2(c/(a + c))
#                     + (a/(a + c)) * log2(a/(a + c)))

# ===== Total Information Entropy for Y =======================
# Outcome uncertainty of Y
HY = -(c + d) * log2(c + d) - (a + b) * log2(a + b)


# ===== Mutual Information ====================================
# Uncertainty reduction in outcome Y due to X
MI = HY - HYgX                           # Mutual Information


# ===== Record direction of relationship (pos or neg) =========
D = ifelse(a + d > b + c, 1, -1)


 # Package Cond Entropy, Mutual Info & Direction for output
Hout = cbind(HY, HYgX, MI, D)
return(Hout)
}                                         # End of Entropy2 Function
```

R Code to Perform Information Analysis for Two Variables at a Time Using the *abcd* Method

References

Acher, C. H., & Snidal, D. (1989). Rational deterrence theory and comparative case studies. *World Politics, 41*(2), 143–169.

Aleksandrov, P. A. (2002). *Akademik Anatolii Petrovich Aleksandrov: Priamaia rech* (2nd ed.). Moscow, Russia: Nauka.

Arrow, K. J. (1996). The economics of information: An exposition. *Empirica, 23*(2), 119–128.

Bailey, K. D. (1994). *Sociology and the new systems theory: Toward a theoretical synthesis.* Albany, NY: SUNY Press.

Bekenstein, J. D. (1973). Black Holes and Entropy. *Physical Review D, 7*(8), 2333–2346.

Bickel, J. E., & Smith, J. E. (2006). Optimal sequential exploration: A binary learning model. *Decision Analysis, 3*(1), 16–32.

Brady, H. E., & Collier, D. (Eds.). (2010). *Rethinking social inquiry: Diverse tools, shared standards* (2nd ed.). Lanham, MD: Rowman & Littlefield.

Brady, H. E., Collier, D., & Seawright, J. (2010). Sources of leverage in causal inference: Toward an alternative view of methodology. In H. E. Brady & D. Collier (Eds.), *Rethinking social inquiry: Diverse tools, shared standards* (2nd ed., pp. 161–200). Lanham, MD: Rowman & Littlefield.

Brown, L. D., Cai, T. T., & DasGupta, A. (2001). Interval estimation for a binomial proportion. *Statistical Science, 16*(2), 101–133.

Bueno de Mesquita, B. (2002). Domestic politics and international relations. *International Studies Quarterly, 46*(1), 1–9.

Cleveland, W. (1993). *Visualizing data.* Summit, NJ: Hobart Press.

Coburn, C., Russell, J., Kaufman, J. H., & Stein, M. K. (2012). Supporting sustainability: Teacher's advice networks and ambitious instructional reform. *American Journal of Education, 119*(1), 137–182.

Cooper, H., Hedges, L. V., & Valentine, J. C. (Eds.). (2009). *The handbook of research synthesis and meta-analysis.* New York, NY: Russell Sage Foundation.

Cover, T. M. (1991). Universal portfolios. *Mathematical Finance, 1*(1), 1–29.

Cover, T. M., & Thomas, J. A. (2006). *Elements of information theory* (2nd ed.). New York, NY: John Wiley.

Creswell, J. W. (2013). *Research design: Qualitative, quantitative, and mixed methods approaches* (4th ed.). Thousand Oaks, CA: Sage.

Donnelly, F., & Wiechula, R. (2013). An example of qualitative comparative analysis in nursing research. *Nurse Researcher, 20*(6), 6–11.

Drozdova, E. (K.) (2008). *Organizations, technology, and network risks: How and why organizations use technology to counter or cloak their human network vulnerabilities* (Doctoral dissertation). Information, Operations, and Management Sciences, New York University.

Drozdova, K., & Gaubatz, K. T. (2014). Reducing uncertainty: Information analysis for comparative case studies. *International Studies Quarterly, 58*(3), 633–645.

Drozdova, K., & Samoilov, M. (2010). Predictive analysis of concealed social network activities based on communication technology choices: Early-warning detection of attack signals from terrorist organizations. *Computational and Mathematical Organization Theory, 16*(1), 61–88.

Dunbar, R., & Starbuck, W. H. (2006). Learning to design organizations and learning from designing them. *Organization Science, 17*(2), 171–178.

Eckstein, H. (1975). Case studies and theory in political science. In F. Greenstein & N. Polsby (Eds.). *Handbook of political science* (Vol. 7, pp. 79–138). Reading, MA: Addison-Wesley.

Esteban, M. D., & Morales, D. (1995). A summary on entropy statistics. *Kybernetika, 31*(4), 337–346.

Gaubatz, K. T. (2015). *A survivor's guide to R: An introduction for the uninitiated and the unnerved.* Thousand Oaks, CA: Sage.

George, A. L., & Bennett, A. (2005). *Case studies and theory development in the social sciences.* Cambridge, MA: MIT Press.

George, A. L., & Simons, W. E. (Eds.). (1994). *The limits of coercive diplomacy* (2nd ed.). Boulder, CO: Westview.

George, A. L., & Smoke, R. (1974). *Deterrence in American foreign policy: Theory and practice.* New York, NY: Columbia University Press.

Gezari, S., Chornock, R., Rest, A., Huber, M. E., Forster, K., Berger, E., . . . Price, P. A. (2012). An ultraviolet–optical flare from the tidal disruption of a helium-rich stellar core. *Nature, 485*(7397), 217–220.

Giffin, A. (2008). *Maximum entropy: The universal method for inference* (Unpublished doctoral dissertation). Albany: Department of Physics, State University of New York.

Gleick, J. (2011). *The information: A history, a theory, a flood.* New York, NY: Pantheon.

Gomm, R., Hammersley, M., & Foster, P. (Eds.). (2000). *Case study method: Key issues, key texts.* London, England: Sage.

Gorard, S. (2013). *Research design: Creating robust approaches for the social sciences.* London, England: Sage.

Gurr, T. R. (1970). *Why men rebel.* Princeton, NJ: Princeton University Press.

Hawking, S. W. (1976). Black holes and thermodynamics. *Physical Review D, 13*(2), 191–197.

Hogeweg, P. (2011). The roots of bioinformatics in theoretical biology. *PLoS Computational Biology, 7*(3), e1002021.

Hogg, R. V., & Craig, A. T. (1995). *Introduction to mathematical statistics* (5th ed.). New York, NY: Prentice Hall.

Holloway, D. (1983). *The Soviet Union and the arms race.* New Haven, CT: Yale University Press.

Horgan, J. (1990). Claude E. Shannon: Unicyclist, juggler and father of information theory. *Scientific American, 262*(1), 22–22B.

Huang, R. (2014). RQDA: R-based qualitative data analysis [Computer program: R package]. Retrieved from http://rqda.r-forge.r-project.org/

Hulley, S., Cummings, R., Browner, W. S., Grady, D. G., & Newman, T. B. (2013). *Designing clinical research* (4th ed.). Philadelphia, PA: Lippincott, Williams & Wilkins.

Jaynes, E. T. (1986). Bayesian methods: General background. In J. H. Justice (Ed.), *Maximum-entropy and Bayesian methods in applied statistics* (pp. 1–25). Cambridge, England: Cambridge University Press.

Johnson, R. B., Onwuegbuzie, A. J., & Turner, L. A. (2007). Toward a definition of mixed methods research. *Journal of Mixed Methods Research, 1*(2), 112–133.

King, G., Keohane, R. O., & Verba, S. (1994). *Designing social inquiry: Scientific inference in qualitative research.* Princeton, NJ: Princeton University Press.

Kittel, C., & Kroemer, H. (1980). *Thermal physics.* New York, NY: Freeman.

Landau, L. D., & Lifshitz, E. M. (1964). *Statisticheskaia Fizika* (2nd ed.). Moscow, USSR: Nauka.

Lijphart, A. (1971). Comparative politics and the comparative method. *American Political Science Review, 65*(3), 682–693.

MacCormick, J. (2013). *Nine algorithms that changed the future: The ingenious ideas that drive today's computers.* Princeton, NJ: Princeton University Press.

Mackie, J. L. (1965). Causes and conditions. *American Philosophical Quarterly, 2*(4), 245–264.

May, M. M. (1985). The U.S.-Soviet approach to nuclear weapons. *International Security, 9*(4), 140–153.

Mill, J. S. (1843). *A system of logic, ratiocinative and inductive: Being a connected view of the principles of evidence and the methods of scientific investigation.* London, England: John W. Parker.

Minerbo, G. N. (1979). MENT: A maximum entropy algorithm for reconstructing a source from projection data. *Computer Graphics and Image Processing, 10*(1), 48–68.

Miranda, M. L., & Aldy, J. E. (1998). Unit pricing of residential municipal solid waste: Lessons from nine case study communities. *Journal of Environmental Management, 52*(1), 79–93.

Nielsen, M. A., & Chuang, I. L. (2000). *Quantum computation and quantum information.* Cambridge, England: Cambridge University Press.

Paninski, L. (2003). Estimation of entropy and mutual information. *Neural Computation, 15*(6), 1191–1253.

Provost, F., & Fawcett, T. (2013). *Data science for business: What you need to know about data mining and data-analytic thinking.* Sebastopol, CA: O'Reilly Media, Inc.

Radner, R. (2000). Costly and bounded rationality in individual and team decision-making. *Industrial and Corporate Change, 9*(4) 623–658. Also published as Radner, R. (2001). Bounded and costly rationality. In N. J. Smelser & P. B. Baltes (Eds.), *International encyclopedia of the social and behavioral sciences* (pp. 1298–1303). Oxford, England: Elsevier Science Ltd.

Ragin, C. (1987). *The comparative method: Moving beyond qualitative and quantitative strategies.* Berkeley: University of California Press.

Ragin, C., & Becker, H. S. (Eds.). (1992). *What is a case? Exploring the foundations of social inquiry.* Cambridge, England: Cambridge University Press.

Ramakrishnan, N., & Bose, R. (2012). Dipole entropy based techniques for segmentation of introns and exons in DNA. *Applied Physics Letter, 101*(8), 083701. Retrieved from http://dx.doi.org/10.1063/1.4747205

Rokkan, S. (1970). *Citizens, elections, parties.* New York, NY: McKay.

Roulston, M. S. (1999). Estimating the errors on measured entropy and mutual information. *Physica D, 125*(3–4), 285–294.

Rudel, T. (2005). *Tropical forests: Regional paths of destruction and regeneration in the late twentieth century.* New York, NY: Columbia University Press.

Samoilov, M., Arkin, A., & Ross, J. (2001). On the deduction of chemical reaction pathways from measurements of time series of concentrations. *Chaos: An Interdisciplinary Journal of Nonlinear Science, 11*(1), 108–114.

Schrödinger, E. (1980). The present situation in quantum mechanics: A translation of Schrodinger's "Cat Paradox' Paper" (J. D. Trimmer, Trans.). *Proceedings of the American Philosophical Society, 124*(5),

323–338. (Original work published 1935 [Schrödinger, E. (1935). Die gegenwärtige situation in der quantenmechanik. *Naturwissenschaften, 23,* 807–812, 823–828, 844–849])

Segal, J. (2008). Shannon, Claude Elwood. In N. Koertge (Ed.), *New dictionary of scientific biography* (pp. 424–430). Detroit, MI: Scribners.

Shannon, C. E. (1948). A mathematical theory of communication. *Bell System Technical Journal, 27*(3–4), 379–423, 623–656. Retrieved from http://www3.alcatel-lucent.com/bstj/vol27–1948/articles/bstj27–3 -379.pdf and http://www3.alcatel-lucent.com/bstj/vol27–1948/articles/bstj27–4-623.pdf

Shannon, C. E., & Weaver, W. (1949). *The mathematical theory of communication.* Urbana: University of Illinois Press.

Sheingate, A. D. (2006). Structure and opportunity: Committee jurisdiction and issue attention in Congress. *American Journal of Political Science, 50*(4), 844–859.

Skinner, K. K., Kudelia, S., Bueno de Mesquita, B., & Rice, C. (2008). *The strategy of campaigning: Lessons from Ronald Reagan and Boris Yeltsin.* Ann Arbor: University of Michigan Press.

Stewart, I. (2012). *In pursuit of the unknown: 17 equations that changed the world.* New York, NY: Basic Books.

Sveshnikov, A. A. (1978). *Problems in probability theory, mathematical statistics and theory of random functions.* New York, NY: Dover.

Thiem, A., & Duşa, A. (2013). *Qualitative comparative analysis with R: A user's guide.* New York, NY: Springer.

Tolman, R. C. (1979). *Principles of statistical mechanics.* Mineola, NY: Dover Publications. (Original work published 1938)

Truss, J. (1999). *Discrete mathematics for computer scientists* (2nd ed.). Harlow, England: Addison Wesley.

Tversky, A., & Kahneman, D. (1974). Judgment under uncertainty: Heuristics and biases. *Science, 185*(4157), 1124–1131.

Van Evera, S. (1997). *Guide to methods for students of political science.* Ithaca, NY: Cornell University Press.

Verdú, S. (1998). Fifty years of Shannon theory. *IEEE Transactions on Information Theory, 44*(6), 2057–2078.

Yin, R. K. (2004). *The case study anthology.* Thousand Oaks, CA: Sage.

Yin, R. K. (2011). *Qualitative research from start to finish.* New York, NY: Guilford.

Yin, R. K. (2014). *Case study research design and methods* (5th ed.). Thousand Oaks, CA: Sage.

Index

Comparative case analysis, truth tables for, 56–61
Comparative case studies, 7–8
Comparative Method, The (Ragin), 118
Complementary methods in research, xix, 1–2, 9,
    12–13, 40–41, 48, 52, 115–129, 131–138.
    See also Multimethod research
Complexity:
    causal, 117, 131
    entropy to represent, 18–23
    uncertainty, and, 7, 18–23
    Computer science, 2, 6, 31, 33, 38
    Conditional information entropy:
    abcd shortcut to, 72
    computing, 68–70
    from explanatory factors and outcome
    variables, 29
    overview, 27
Conditional probabilities:
    abcd method and, 26–27
    calculating, 61–63, 66–67
    information metrics from, 145–147
    outcome uncertainty measure, 27–28
    overview, 26–27
Confidence intervals, information metrics and,
    101–102
Confidence levels, 39
"Contingent generalization," 38, 41–42.
    See also "Analytic generalization," Modest
    generalization"
Cooper, H., xx
Correspondence, classic methods of, 115
Counterfactual analysis, 115
Cover, T., 32–33
"Coverage," in QCA, 116
Craig, A., 24
Creswell, J. 53
Crisp-set QCA, 115. *See also* Qualitative case
    analysis (QCA)
Cross-national theory of campaigning, 47
Cryptography, Information theory and, 4, 6, 7, 17, 31
Cyber, cyberspace, cyber/information security, cyber
    war, xxv, 18, 134, 135

DasGupta, A., 14
Data compression, 32–33, 133–134
Dependent (outcome) variables:
    analysis of, 99-102
    coding, 56–59, 110–112

confidence intervals, and, 102
explanatory factors, as, 7, 10, 27, 73
extreme values, 45
independent variable, relationship to, 14, 27–32,
    51, 68, 113, 134–135
information entropy of, 22, 28–32, 73,
    99–100, 142
probability, and, 24–27, 140
qualitative case analysis (QCA), and,
    115–117, 134
research design, and, 10, 22, 38, 41, 47,
    50–51, 55
selecting cases on, 51–52
statistical independence, 32
uncertainty, and, 6, 27, 73
variation, lack of, 52
See also, Binary coding of variables, Coding,
    Independent variables, Truth tables
Digital revolution, 18, 99. *See also* "Information
    revolution"
Direction, in uncertainty measurement, 28, 30–31,
    71–72, 86
DNA encoding, information theory and, 34
Donnelly, F., 92
Dot charts, 106
Dropped-case analysis, 106–110
Drozdova, K., 34, 48, 51
Dunbar, R., 44
Dușa, A., 128–129

Eckstein, H., 48, 100, 136
Economics, information theory and, 34
Elements of Information Theory
    (Cover and Thomas), 32
Entropy, 18–23, 138. *See also* Information entropy
Environmental incentives study, 102–105
EPA (U.S. Environmental Protection Agency), 102
Error. *See* Sensitivity analysis
Esteban, M., 101
Ethnic mobilization data, 118–122
Evidence and logic, in research design, 40–41
Excel, information metrics in, 24, 106, 139–143
Experimentation, 39, 42, 46, 48, 57, 87
Explanatory factors. *See* Independent variables
Exponentiation, 23–24

Fawcett, T., 34
Foster, P., 44

Gaubatz, K. T., 51, 106, 145
George, A.:
  binary outcome coding, 33
  case cumulation, 44
  contingent generalization, 38–39, 41, 100
  deterrence theory, 34
  Limits of Coercive Diplomacy, 55, 58–59, 77, 139
  "most likely" and "least likely" cases, 100
  structured, focused comparison method, 5–6,
    9–10, 12–13, 52, 137
Giffin, A., 138
Gleick, James, 2
Gomm, R., 44
Gorard, S., 53
Grady, D., 53
Gurr, T., 117

Hammersley, M., 44
Hawking, S., 19
Hedges, L., xx
Hogeweg, P., 34
Hogg, R., 24
Holloway, D., 34
Horgan, J., 17
Huang, R., 145
Hulley, S., 53
Hybrid research designs (experiments and
    observations), 39
Hybrid security threats, 135
Hypothesis testing, 12, 38–39

Independent variables:
  analysis of, 99–100
  coding, 56–59
  comparing, 43, 73, 76, 86–87, 91–92, 96–97,
    104, 108, 129
  confidence intervals, and, 102
  dependent variable, relationship to, 14, 27–32,
    51, 68, 113, 134–135
  explanatory factors, as, 7, 10, 27, 73
  extreme values, 45
  information entropy, and, 28–32, 73,
    99–100, 142
  probability, and, 24–27, 140
  qualitative case analysis (QCA), and,
    115–117, 134
  research design, and, 10, 22, 38, 41, 47,
    50–51, 55

statistical independence, 28, 32
variation, lack of, 52
See also, Binary coding of variables, Coding,
    Dependent variables, Truth tables
Inference, 4, 8–9, 41–45, 48, 50, 105, 136
Inferential leverage, 100
Information, The (Gleick), 2
Information Age, and beyond, xxii, 1–5, 17, 32, 99,
    135, 138
Information entropy:
  information method, 68, 72
  information theory, 6–8, 13–14, 17–23, 27–30,
    31–34
  minimum descriptive complexity of random
    variables, 32
  mutual information based on, 14, 30
  origins in physics, xxii, 4, 6, 8, 18–21,
    33–34, 38
  Shannon's development of, 2, 8
  uncertainty measure, 27–29
Information method, 55–78
  advantages of, xix, 3, 14, 37, 42-43, 100, 101,
    113, 129, 133–137
  calculating probabilities, 61–67
  implementing, 11, 55–78, 74–75 (figure)
  outcome comparisons, 73–77
  truth tables for comparative case analysis,
    56–61
  uncertainty measure computations, 67–73,
    74–75 (figure)
Information metrics, 11, 79–98, 131–135
  abcd method, 72, 74–75 (figure), 89–91, 95–96,
    148–149
  accounting for teaching quality case, 88–92
  advantages of, 131–135
  conditional probabilities, and, 145–147
  confidence intervals and, 101–102
  Excel for, 139–143
  qualitative case analysis (QCA) *compared to*,
    117–118
  R computer language for, 145–149
  structured-focused comparison and, 52
Information perspective in case selection, 45
Information revolution, 17–36, 131, 134
  information theory in, 17–23, 33–34
  Shannon's contribution to, 131
Information sources, combining, 7, 31–33,
    134–135